D1279817

Regional Integration

Integrating National Economies: Promise and Pitfalls

Barry Bosworth (Brookings Institution) and Gur Ofer (Hebrew University)
Reforming Planned Economies in an Integrating World Economy

Ralph C. Bryant (Brookings Institution)
International Coordination of National Stabilization Policies

Susan M. Collins (Brookings Institution/Georgetown University)
Distributive Issues: A Constraint on Global Integration

Richard N. Cooper (Harvard University)
Environment and Resource Policies for the World Economy

Ronald G. Ehrenberg (Cornell University)
Labor Markets and Integrating National Economies

Barry Eichengreen (University of California, Berkeley)
International Monetary Arrangements for the 21st Century

Mitsuhiro Fukao (Bank of Japan)
Financial Integration, Corporate Governance, and the Performance of Multinational Companies

Stephan Haggard (University of California, San Diego)
Developing Nations and the Politics of Global Integration

Richard J. Herring (University of Pennsylvania) and Robert E. Litan (Department of Justice/Brookings Institution)
Financial Regulation in the Global Economy

Miles Kahler (University of California, San Diego)
International Institutions and the Political Economy of Integration

Anne O. Krueger (Stanford University)
Trade Policies and Developing Nations

Robert Z. Lawrence (Harvard University)
Regionalism, Multilateralism, and Deeper Integration

Sylvia Ostry (University of Toronto) and Richard R. Nelson (Columbia University)
Techno-Nationalism and Techno-Globalism: Conflict and Cooperation

Robert L. Paarlberg (Wellesley College/Harvard University)
Leadership Abroad Begins at Home: U.S. Foreign Economic Policy after the Cold War

Peter Rutland (Wesleyan University)
Russia, Eurasia, and the Global Economy

F. M. Scherer (Harvard University)
Competition Policies for an Integrated World Economy

Susan L. Shirk (University of California, San Diego)
How China Opened Its Door: The Political Success of the PRC's Foreign Trade and Investment Reforms

Alan O. Sykes (University of Chicago)
Product Standards for Internationally Integrated Goods Markets

Akihiko Tanaka (Institute of Oriental Culture, University of Tokyo)
The Politics of Deeper Integration: National Attitudes and Policies in Japan

Vito Tanzi (International Monetary Fund)
Taxation in an Integrating World

William Wallace (St. Antony's College, Oxford University)
Regional Integration: The West European Experience

William Wallace

Regional Integration: The West European Experience

THE BROOKINGS INSTITUTION
Washington, D.C.

Copyright © 1994
THE BROOKINGS INSTITUTION
1775 Massachusetts Avenue, N. W., Washington, D.C. 20036

Library of Congress Cataloging-in-Publication data:
Wallace, William, 1927–
Regional integration: the West European experience/William Wallace
p. cm. — (Integrating national economies)
Includes bibliographical references and index.
ISBN 0-8157-9224-7. — ISBN 0-8157-9223-9 (pbk.)
1. Europe—Economic integration. I. Title. II. Series.
HC241.W35 1994
337. 1′4—dc20   94-23160
                                                              CIP

9 8 7 6 5 4 3 2 1

The paper used in this publication meets the minimum requirements of
American National Standard for Information Sciences—Permanence of Paper
for Printed Library Materials, ANSI Z39.48-1984

Typeset in Plantin

Composition by Princeton Editorial Associates
Princeton, New Jersey

Printed by R. R. Donnelley and Sons Co.
Harrisonburg, Virginia

Foreword

THE European Community (officially the European Union since the ratification of the Maastricht Treaty in 1993) is the oldest and most highly developed example of institutionalized regional integration. Starting with the integration of markets for coal and steel among six countries in the early 1950s, the EU has moved from the shallow integration of dismantling trade barriers to the deep integration of common policies on agriculture, environment, transport, and working conditions. It has also accepted common rules on competition and mergers and financial transfers through a common budget. The law of the EU is directly applied in the domestic courts of member states. The governments and administrations of the member states interact intensively on a range of domestic policies. Attitudes toward further European integration are a major issue in the domestic politics of most member states.

Over the past forty years the EU has also expanded, from its initial six members to nine in 1973 and twelve in 1986. Austria, Finland, Sweden, and Norway completed negotiations for entry in early 1994, to bring membership—subject to approval through popular referenda—to sixteen in January 1995. Following the transformation of East European regimes in 1989–90, a lengthening queue of applicants for the privileges of membership now stretches across central, southeastern, and eastern Europe, raising the prospect that this regional organization will approach twenty-five to thirty member states within the next decade.

Any study of the integration of national economies must therefore pay attention to the West European experience. How far should those promoting regional integration in the Western Hemisphere and the Pacific look to the EU as a model? Do the evolution of a common commercial policy within the EU and moves toward common foreign and security policies suggest that regional and global integration can proceed harmoniously in parallel? Or will tensions between regional and global priorities unavoidably arise?

This volume emphasizes the historical circumstances under which the institutions of West European integration were established. Successful establishment and enlargement of institutionalized regional integration required heavy political and military investment by American administrations over several decades, justified by the clear and present danger of a Soviet-Communist advance into the region. This was accompanied by equally heavy and long-term political investment in reconciling Germany—the potential regional hegemon—with its neighbors, and in building political and legal institutions with the capacity to override national governments and national laws. If the nations in the North American Free Trade Agreement, the Asia-Pacific Economic Cooperation group, or other regional groupings are ever to move beyond shallow initial agreements to the deep integration of common rules impartially implemented, it is argued, they will have to grapple with similar issues of sovereignty, political commitment, and regional balance.

William Wallace would like to thank participants in a working conference at the Brookings Institution in January 1994 for comments on an early draft of this paper, and also Suzanne Berger, Simon Bulmer, Noriki Hirose, Stanley Hoffmann, Pietro Nivola, Julie Smith, and Helen Wallace for written comments and criticisms. He would also like to thank Philip Budden, Anthony Forster, Jeff Stacey, Stefan Talmon, and the staff of the libraries of the Royal Institute of International Affairs (London) and of St. Antony's College, Oxford, for their invaluable help in checking dates, statistics, references, and half-remembered events.

Princeton Editorial Associates edited the manuscript and prepared the index, and David Bearce verified the volume's factual content.

Funding for the project came from the Center for Global Partnership of the Japan Foundation, the Curry Foundation, the Ford Foundation, the Korea Foundation, the Tokyo Club Foundation for Global Studies, the United States–Japan Foundation, and the Alex C. Walker Educational and Charitable Foundation. The author and Brookings are grateful for their support.

The views expressed in this book are those of the author and should not be ascribed to the persons or organizations whose assistance is acknowledged or to the trustees, officers, or staff members of the Brookings Institution.

BRUCE K. MACLAURY
President

November 1994
Washington, D.C.

Contents

Abbreviations and Acronyms

APEC	Asia-Pacific Economic Cooperation
CAP	Common Agricultural Policy
CFSP	Common Foreign and Security Policy
CSCE	Conference on Security and Cooperation in Europe
EC	European Community
ECJ	European Court of Justice
Ecosoc	Economic and Social Committee
ECSC	European Coal and Steel Community
EDC	European Defence Community
EEA	European Economic Area
EEC	European Economic Community
EFTA	European Free Trade Association
EMS	European Monetary System
EMU	economic and monetary union
EPC	European Political Cooperation
EU	European Union
Euratom	European Atomic Energy Community
GATT	General Agreement on Tariffs and Trade
GDP	gross domestic production
G7	Group of Seven
IEA	International Energy Agency
IGC	Intergovernmental Conference
IMF	International Monetary Fund
NACC	NATO Consultative Committee
NAFTA	North American Free Trade Agreement

NATO	North Atlantic Treaty Organization
OECD	Organization for Economic Cooperation and Development
OEEC	Organization for European Economic Cooperation
WEU	West European Union

Preface to the Studies on Integrating National Economies

ECONOMIC interdependence among nations has increased sharply in the past half century. For example, while the value of total production of industrial countries increased at a rate of about 9 percent a year on average between 1964 and 1992, the value of the exports of those nations grew at an average rate of 12 percent, and lending and borrowing across national borders through banks surged upward even more rapidly at 23 percent a year. This international economic interdependence has contributed to significantly improved standards of living for most countries. Continuing international economic integration holds out the promise of further benefits. Yet the increasing sensitivity of national economies to events and policies originating abroad creates dilemmas and pitfalls if national policies and international cooperation are poorly managed.

The Brookings Project on Integrating National Economies, of which this study is a component, focuses on the interplay between two fundamental facts about the world at the end of the twentieth century. First, the world will continue for the foreseeable future to be organized politically into nation-states with sovereign governments. Second, increasing economic integration among nations will continue to erode differences among national economies and undermine the autonomy of national governments. The project explores the opportunities and tensions arising from these two facts.

Scholars from a variety of disciplines have produced twenty-one studies for the first phase of the project. Each study examines the heightened competition between national political sovereignty and increased cross-border economic integration. This preface identifies background themes and issues common to all the studies and provides a brief overview of the project as a whole.[1]

Increasing World Economic Integration

Two underlying sets of causes have led nations to become more closely intertwined. First, technological, social, and cultural changes have sharply reduced the effective economic distances among nations. Second, many of the government policies that traditionally inhibited cross-border transactions have been relaxed or even dismantled.

The same improvements in transportation and communications technology that make it much easier and cheaper for companies in New York to ship goods to California, for residents of Strasbourg to visit relatives in Marseilles, and for investors in Hokkaido to buy and sell shares on the Tokyo Stock Exchange facilitate trade, migration, and capital movements spanning nations and continents. The sharply reduced costs of moving goods, money, people, and information underlie the profound economic truth that technology has made the world markedly smaller.

New communications technology has been especially significant for financial activity. Computers, switching devices, and telecommunications satellites have slashed the cost of transmitting information internationally, of confirming transactions, and of paying for transactions. In the 1950s, for example, foreign exchange could be bought and sold only during conventional business hours in the initiating party's time zone. Such transactions can now be carried out instantaneously twenty-four hours a day. Large banks pass the management of their worldwide foreign-exchange positions around the globe from one branch to another, staying continuously ahead of the setting sun.

Such technological innovations have increased the knowledge of potentially profitable international exchanges and of economic opportunities abroad. Those developments, in turn, have changed consumers' and producers' tastes. Foreign goods, foreign vacations, foreign financial investments—virtually anything from other nations—have lost some of their exotic character.

1. A complete list of authors and study titles is included at the beginning of this volume, facing the title page.

Although technological change permits increased contact among nations, it would not have produced such dramatic effects if it had been countermanded by government policies. Governments have traditionally taxed goods moving in international trade, directly restricted imports and subsidized exports, and tried to limit international capital movements. Those policies erected "separation fences" at the borders of nations. From the perspective of private sector agents, separation fences imposed extra costs on cross-border transactions. They reduced trade and, in some cases, eliminated it. During the 1930s governments used such policies with particular zeal, a practice now believed to have deepened and lengthened the Great Depression.

After World War II, most national governments began—sometimes unilaterally, more often collaboratively—to lower their separation fences, to make them more permeable, or sometimes even to tear down parts of them. The multilateral negotiations under the auspices of the General Agreement on Trade and Tariffs (GATT)—for example, the Kennedy Round in the 1960s, the Tokyo Round in the 1970s, and most recently the protracted negotiations of the Uruguay Round, formally signed only in April 1994—stand out as the most prominent examples of fence lowering for trade in goods. Though contentious and marked by many compromises, the GATT negotiations are responsible for sharp reductions in at-the-border restrictions on trade in goods and services. After the mid-1980s a large number of developing countries moved unilaterally to reduce border barriers and to pursue outwardly oriented policies.

The lowering of fences for financial transactions began later and was less dramatic. Nonetheless, by the 1990s government restrictions on capital flows, especially among the industrial countries, were much less important and widespread than at the end of World War II and in the 1950s.

By shrinking the economic distances among nations, changes in technology would have progressively integrated the world economy even in the absence of reductions in governments' separation fences. Reductions in separation fences would have enhanced interdependence even without the technological innovations. Together, these two sets of evolutionary changes have reinforced each other and strikingly transformed the world economy.

Changes in the Government of Nations

Simultaneously with the transformation of the global economy, major changes have occurred in the world's political structure. First, the number of governmental decisionmaking units in the world has expanded markedly and political power has been diffused more broadly among them. Rising nationalism and, in some areas, heightened ethnic tensions have accompanied that increasing political pluralism.

The history of membership in international organizations documents the sharp growth in the number of independent states. For example, only 44 nations participated in the Bretton Woods conference of July 1944, which gave birth to the International Monetary Fund. But by the end of 1970, the IMF had 118 member nations. The number of members grew to 150 by the mid-1980s and to 178 by December 1993. Much of this growth reflects the collapse of colonial empires. Although many nations today are small and carry little individual weight in the global economy, their combined influence is considerable and their interests cannot be ignored as easily as they were in the past.

A second political trend, less visible but equally important, has been the gradual loss of the political and economic hegemony of the United States. Immediately after World War II, the United States by itself accounted for more than one-third of world production. By the early 1990s the U.S. share had fallen to about one-fifth. Concurrently, the political and economic influence of the European colonial powers continued to wane, and the economic significance of nations outside Europe and North America, such as Japan, Korea, Indonesia, China, Brazil, and Mexico, increased. A world in which economic power and influence are widely diffused has displaced a world in which one or a few nations effectively dominated international decisionmaking.

Turmoil and the prospect of fundamental change in the formerly centrally planned economies compose a third factor causing radical changes in world politics. During the era of central planning, governments in those nations tried to limit external influences on their economies. Now leaders in the formerly planned economies are trying to adopt reforms modeled on Western capitalist principles. To the extent that these efforts succeed, those nations will increase their economic involvement with the rest of the world. Political and economic alignments among the Western industrialized nations will be forced to adapt.

Governments and scholars have begun to assess these three trends, but their far-reaching ramifications will not be clear for decades.

Dilemmas for National Policies

Cross-border economic integration and national political sovereignty have increasingly come into conflict, leading to a growing mismatch between the economic and political structures of the world. The effective domains of economic markets have come to coincide less and less with national governmental jurisdictions.

When the separation fences at nations' borders were high, governments and citizens could sharply distinguish "international" from "domestic" policies. International policies dealt with at-the-border barriers, such as tariffs and quotas, or responded to events occurring abroad. In contrast, domestic policies were concerned with everything behind the nation's borders, such as competition and antitrust rules, corporate governance, product standards, worker safety, regulation and supervision of financial institutions, environmental protection, tax codes, and the government's budget. Domestic policies were regarded as matters about which nations were sovereign, to be determined by the preferences of the nation's citizens and its political institutions, without regard for effects on other nations.

As separation fences have been lowered and technological innovations have shrunk economic distances, a multitude of formerly neglected differences among nations' domestic policies have become exposed to international scrutiny. National governments and international negotiations must thus increasingly deal with "deeper"—behind-the-border—integration. For example, if country A permits companies to emit air and water pollutants whereas country B does not, companies that use pollution-generating methods of production will find it cheaper to produce in country A. Companies in country B that compete internationally with companies in country A are likely to complain that foreign competitors enjoy unfair advantages and to press for international pollution standards.

Deeper integration requires analysis of the economic and the political aspects of virtually all nonborder policies and practices. Such issues have already figured prominently in negotiations over the evolution of the European Community, over the Uruguay Round of GATT negotiations, over the North American Free Trade Agreement (NAFTA), and over the bilateral economic relationships between Japan and the United States. Future debates about behind-the-border policies will occur with increasing frequency and prove at least as complex and contentious as the past negotiations regarding at-the-border restrictions.

Tensions about deeper integration arise from three broad sources: cross-border spillovers, diminished national autonomy, and challenges to political sovereignty.

Cross-Border Spillovers

Some activities in one nation produce consequences that spill across borders and affect other nations. Illustrations of these spillovers abound. Given the impact of modern technology of banking and securities markets in creating interconnected networks, lax rules in one nation erode the ability of all other nations to enforce banking and securities rules and to deal with fraudulent transactions. Given the rapid diffusion of knowledge, science and technology policies in one nation generate knowledge that other nations can use without full payment. Labor market policies become matters of concern to other nations because workers migrate in search of work; policies in one nation can trigger migration that floods or starves labor markets elsewhere. When one nation dumps pollutants into the air or water that other nations breathe or drink, the matter goes beyond the unitary concern of the polluting nation and becomes a matter for international negotiation. Indeed, the hydrocarbons that are emitted into the atmosphere when individual nations burn coal for generating electricity contribute to global warming and are thereby a matter of concern for the entire world.

The tensions associated with cross-border spillovers can be especially vexing when national policies generate outcomes alleged to be competitively inequitable, as in the example in which country A permits companies to emit pollutants and country B does not. Or consider a situation in which country C requires commodities, whether produced at home or abroad, to meet certain design standards, justified for safety reasons. Foreign competitors may find it too expensive to meet these standards. In that event, the standards in C act very much like tariffs or quotas, effectively narrowing or even eliminating foreign competition for domestic producers. Citing examples of this sort, producers or governments in individual nations often complain that business is not conducted on a "level playing field." Typically, the complaining nation proposes that *other* nations adjust their policies to moderate or remove the competitive inequities.

Arguments for creating a level playing field are troublesome at best. International trade occurs precisely because of differences among nations—in resource endowments, labor skills, and consumer tastes. Nations specialize in producing goods and services in which they are relatively most efficient. In a fundamental sense, cross-border trade is valuable because the playing field is *not* level.

When David Ricardo first developed the theory of comparative advantage, he focused on differences among nations owing to climate or technology. But Ricardo could as easily have ascribed the productive differences to differing "social climates" as to physical or technological climates. Taking all "climatic" differences as given, the theory of comparative advantage argues that free trade among nations will maximize global welfare.

Taken to its logical extreme, the notion of leveling the playing field implies that nations should become homogeneous in all major respects. But that recommendation is unrealistic and even pernicious. Suppose country A decides that it is too poor to afford the costs of a clean environment, and will thus permit the production of goods that pollute local air and water supplies. Or suppose it concludes that it cannot afford stringent protections for worker safety. Country A will then argue that it is inappropriate for other nations to impute to country A the value they themselves place on a clean environment and safety standards (just as it would be inappropriate to impute the A valuations to the environment of other nations). The core of the idea of political sovereignty is to permit national residents to order their lives and property in accord with their own preferences.

Which perspective about differences among nations in behind-the-border policies is more compelling? Is country A merely exercising its national preferences and appropriately exploiting its comparative advantage in goods that are dirty or dangerous to produce? Or does a legitimate international problem exist that justifies pressure from other nations urging country A to accept changes in its policies (thus

curbing its national sovereignty)? When national governments negotiate resolutions to such questions—trying to agree whether individual
nations are legitimately exercising sovereign choices or, alternatively,
engaging in behavior that is unfair or damaging to other nations—the
dialogue is invariably contentious because the resolutions depend on
the typically complex circumstances of the international spillovers
and on the relative weights accorded to the interests of particular
individuals and particular nations.

Diminished National Autonomy

As cross-border economic integration increases, governments experience greater difficulties in trying to control events within their
borders. Those difficulties, summarized by the term *diminished autonomy*, are the second set of reasons why tensions arise from the competition between political sovereignty and economic integration.

For example, nations adjust monetary and fiscal policies to influence domestic inflation and employment. In setting these policies,
smaller countries have always been somewhat constrained by foreign
economic events and policies. Today, however, all nations are constrained, often severely. More than in the past, therefore, nations may
be better able to achieve their economic goals if they work together
collaboratively in adjusting their macroeconomic policies.

Diminished autonomy and cross-border spillovers can sometimes
be allowed to persist without explicit international cooperation to
deal with them. States in the United States adopt their own tax
systems and set policies for assistance to poor single people without
any formal cooperation or limitation. Market pressures operate to
force a degree of de facto cooperation. If one state taxes corporations
too heavily, it knows business will move elsewhere. (Those familiar
with older debates about "fiscal federalism" within the United States
and other nations will recognize the similarity between those issues
and the emerging international debates about deeper integration of
national economies.) Analogously, differences among nations in regulations, standards, policies, institutions, and even social and cultural
preferences create economic incentives for a kind of arbitrage that
erodes or eliminates the differences. Such pressures involve not only
the conventional arbitrage that exploits price differentials (buying at
one point in geographic space or time and selling at another) but also

shifts in the location of production facilities and in the residence of factors of production.

In many other cases, however, cross-border spillovers, arbitrage pressures, and diminished effectiveness of national policies can produce unwanted consequences. In cases involving what economists call externalities (external economies and diseconomies), national governments may need to cooperate to promote mutual interests. For example, population growth, continued urbanization, and the more intensive exploitation of natural resources generate external diseconomies not only within but across national boundaries. External economies generated when benefits spill across national jurisdictions probably also increase in importance (for instance, the gains from basic research and from control of communicable diseases).

None of these situations is new, but technological change and the reduction of tariffs and quotas heighten their importance. When one nation produces goods (such as scientific research) or "bads" (such as pollution) that significantly affect other nations, individual governments acting sequentially and noncooperatively cannot deal effectively with the resulting issues. In the absence of explicit cooperation and political leadership, too few collective goods and too many collective bads will be supplied.

Challenges to Political Sovereignty

The pressures from cross-border economic integration sometimes even lead individuals or governments to challenge the core assumptions of national political sovereignty. Such challenges are a third source of tensions about deeper integration.

The existing world system of nation-states assumes that a nation's residents are free to follow their own values and to select their own political arrangements without interference from others. Similarly, property rights are allocated by nation. (The so-called global commons, such as outer space and the deep seabed, are the sole exceptions.) A nation is assumed to have the sovereign right to exploit its property in accordance with its own preferences and policies. Political sovereignty is thus analogous to the concept of consumer sovereignty (the presumption that the individual consumer best knows his or her own interests and should exercise them freely).

In times of war, some nations have had sovereignty wrested from them by force. In earlier eras, a handful of individuals or groups have questioned the premises of political sovereignty. With the profound increases in economic integration in recent decades, however, a larger number of individuals and groups—and occasionally even their national governments—have identified circumstances in which, it is claimed, some universal or international set of values should take precedence over the preferences or policies of particular nations.

Some groups seize on human-rights issues, for example, or what they deem to be egregiously inappropriate political arrangements in other nations. An especially prominent case occurred when citizens in many nations labeled the former apartheid policies of South Africa an affront to universal values and emphasized that the South African government was not legitimately representing the interests of a majority of South Africa's residents. Such views caused many national governments to apply economic sanctions against South Africa. Examples of value conflicts are not restricted to human rights, however. Groups focusing on environmental issues characterize tropical rain forests as the lungs of the world and the genetic repository for numerous species of plants and animals that are the heritage of all mankind. Such views lead Europeans, North Americans, or Japanese to challenge the timber-cutting policies of Brazilians and Indonesians. A recent controversy over tuna fishing with long drift nets that kill porpoises is yet another example. Environmentalists in the United States whose sensibilities were offended by the drowning of porpoises required U.S. boats at some additional expense to amend their fishing practices. The U.S. fishermen, complaining about imported tuna caught with less regard for porpoises, persuaded the U.S. government to ban such tuna imports (both direct imports from the countries in which the tuna is caught and indirect imports shipped via third countries). Mexico and Venezuela were the main countries affected by this ban; a GATT dispute panel sided with Mexico against the United States in the controversy, which further upset the U.S. environmental community.

A common feature of all such examples is the existence, real or alleged, of "psychological externalities" or "political failures." Those holding such views reject untrammeled political sovereignty for nation-states in deference to universal or non-national values. They wish to constrain the exercise of individual nations' sovereignties through international negotiations or, if necessary, by even stronger intervention.

The Management of International Convergence

In areas in which arbitrage pressures and cross-border spillovers are weak and psychological or political externalities are largely absent, national governments may encounter few problems with deeper integration. Diversity across nations may persist quite easily. But at the other extreme, arbitrage and spillovers in some areas may be so strong that they threaten to erode national diversity completely. Or psychological and political sensitivities may be asserted too powerfully to be ignored. Governments will then be confronted with serious tensions, and national policies and behaviors may eventually converge to common, worldwide patterns (for example, subject to internationally agreed norms or minimum standards). Eventual convergence across nations, if it occurs, could happen in a harmful way (national policies and practices being driven to a least common denominator with externalities ignored, in effect a "race to the bottom") or it could occur with mutually beneficial results ("survival of the fittest and the best").

Each study in this series addresses basic questions about the management of international convergence: if, when, and how national governments should intervene to try to influence the consequences of arbitrage pressures, cross-border spillovers, diminished autonomy, and the assertion of psychological or political externalities. A wide variety of responses is conceivable. We identify six, which should be regarded not as distinct categories but as ranges along a continuum.

National autonomy defines a situation at one end of the continuum in which national governments make decentralized decisions with little or no consultation and no explicit cooperation. This response represents political sovereignty at its strongest, undiluted by any international management of convergence.

Mutual recognition, like national autonomy, presumes decentralized decisions by national governments and relies on market competition to guide the process of international convergence. Mutual recognition, however, entails exchanges of information and consultations among governments to constrain the formation of national regulations and policies. As understood in discussions of economic integration within the European Community, moreover, mutual recognition entails an explicit acceptance by each member nation of the regulations, standards, and certification procedures of other members. For example, mutual recognition allows wine or liquor produced in any European Union country to be sold in all twelve member countries even if production standards in member countries differ. Doctors licensed in France are permitted to practice in Germany, and vice versa, even if licensing procedures in the two countries differ.

Governments may agree on rules that restrict their freedom to set policy or that promote gradual convergence in the structure of policy. As international consultations and monitoring of compliance with such rules become more important, this situation can be described as *monitored decentralization*. The Group of Seven finance ministers meetings, supplemented by the IMF's surveillance over exchange rate and macroeconomic policies, illustrate this approach to management.

Coordination goes further than mutual recognition and monitored decentralization in acknowledging convergence pressures. It is also more ambitious in promoting intergovernmental cooperation to deal with them. Coordination involves jointly designed mutual adjustments of national policies. In clear-cut cases of coordination, bargaining occurs and governments agree to behave differently from the ways they would have behaved without the agreement. Examples include the World Health Organization's procedures for controlling communicable diseases and the 1987 Montreal Protocol (to a 1985 framework convention) for the protection of stratospheric ozone by reducing emissions of chlorofluorocarbons.

Explicit harmonization, which requires still higher levels of intergovernmental cooperation, may require agreement on regional standards or world standards. Explicit harmonization typically entails still greater departures from decentralization in decisionmaking and still further strengthening of international institutions. The 1988 agreement among major central banks to set minimum standards for the required capital positions of commercial banks (reached through the Committee on Banking Regulations and Supervisory Practices at the Bank for International Settlements) is an example of partially harmonized regulations.

At the opposite end of the spectrum from national autonomy lies *federalist mutual governance*, which implies continuous bargaining and joint, centralized decisionmaking. To make federalist mutual governance work would require greatly strengthened supranational institutions. This end of the management spectrum, now relevant only as an analytical benchmark, is a possible outcome that can be imagined for the middle or late decades of the twenty-first century, possibly even sooner for regional groupings like the European Union.

Overview of the Brookings Project

Despite their growing importance, the issues of deeper economic integration and its competition with national political sovereignty were largely neglected in the 1980s. In 1992 the Brookings Institution initiated its project on Integrating National Economies to direct attention to these important questions.

In studying this topic, Brookings sought and received the co-operation of some of the world's leading economists, political scientists, foreign-policy specialists, and government officials, representing all regions of the world. Although some functional areas require a special focus on European, Japanese, and North American perspectives, at all junctures the goal was to include, in addition, the perspectives of developing nations and the formerly centrally planned economies.

The first phase of the project commissioned the twenty-one scholarly studies listed at the beginning of the book. One or two lead discussants, typically residents of parts of the world other than the area where the author resides, were asked to comment on each study.

Authors enjoyed substantial freedom to design their individual studies, taking due account of the overall themes and goals of the project. The guidelines for the studies requested that at least some of the analysis be carried out with a non-normative perspective. In effect, authors were asked to develop a "baseline" of what might happen in the absence of changed policies or further international cooperation. For their normative analyses, authors were asked to start with an agnostic posture that did not prejudge the net benefits or costs resulting from integration. The project organizers themselves had no presumption about whether national diversity is better or worse than international convergence or about what the individual studies should conclude regarding the desirability of increased integration. On the contrary, each author was asked to address the trade-offs in his or her issue area between diversity and convergence and to locate the area, currently and prospectively, on

the spectrum of international management possibilities running between national autonomy through mutual recognition to coordination
and explicit harmonization.

HENRY J. AARON   SUSAN M. COLLINS
RALPH C. BRYANT   ROBERT Z. LAWRENCE

Regional Integration

Chapter 1

Introduction

WEST EUROPEAN integration represents the archetype of regional integration: the only experiment in formal, institutionalized integration above the level of the nation-state to have survived and strengthened from the optimistic days of the early 1960s to the present. Even in the 1960s it was the model that others attempted to follow, around which theories of regional integration were formed that were intended for universal application.[1] The East African Common Market has disappeared without a trace. Early attempts at Latin American integration, on which so many hopes of greater independence from U.S. hegemony were pinned, have given way to smaller subregional groupings and to pursuit of integration with North America. The Council for Mutual Economic Assistance, the socialist countries' experiment in regional integration, collapsed with the socialist bloc—having never moved beyond the shallowest integration of trade among national command economies.

The European Community (EC) is thus the only example to which the student of international integration can turn of a deliberate attempt over an extended period to foster the conditions for deep integration and to create the political institutions for their management. This volume is addressed in particular to those seeking lessons to learn and problems to avoid, in moving toward regional integration in the 1990s in East Asia, North America, and more broadly within the Western Hemisphere. It notes the particular historical and political circumstances in which the institutions and structures of West

---

1. Haas (1961).

1

European integration were established, forty years ago. It emphasizes that these structures were put in place *before* technological advance had created the conditions for deep international economic integration. The Treaties of Paris and Rome were designed to remove barriers between economies still heavily dependent on farming for national prosperity, their steel industries the focus for national industrial strategies, their coal mines the main source of energy. Their rules and competences have had to be adapted, through successive revisions of the treaties as well as through continuous multilateral negotiation, to the transformation of the regional and global economy in the course of the 1970s and 1980s.

The integration of Western Europe was, however, driven not only by economic objectives but also by overriding political and security concerns. Economic integration was a strategy to achieve political objectives: American, French, Dutch, Italian, German. American commitment, American political and financial support, and American provision of security were all important to its establishment and sustainability. French and Dutch recognition of those countries' vulnerability to a reviving Germany complemented German and Italian pursuit of a multilateral framework for their own insecurely rebuilt democracies and for their conditionally regained sovereignty, within which they could pursue a cautiously redefined foreign policy. Democratic societies, rebuilt on the ruins of World War II, were to be secured by linking their governments and economies, and stabilized by the economic growth that regional integration would stimulate. Popular acceptance of integration was eased by recognition of a degree of shared values and cultural community among the mainly Catholic countries of the original Six, and by their common postwar socialization into "Western" values under the influence of their American hegemon.

The boundaries of regional integration in Western Europe—and of Western Europe as a political, economic, and social space—were set by the cold war and by the division of Europe between an American-led western alliance (with a periphery of neutral market democracies under its effective protection) and a Soviet-dominated Warsaw Pact. The conditions for full participation were similarly political as well as economic. West European integration brought together fully democratic political systems, "resolved by thus pooling their resources to preserve and strengthen peace and liberty, and calling upon the other peoples of Europe who share their ideal to join in their efforts."[2] Authoritarian Spain was thus excluded from participation in West European institutions until after the transition from authoritarian to democratic government; authoritarian Portugal, accepted into the Atlantic Alliance because of the strategic importance of its Atlantic islands, nevertheless remained a partial pariah state until after the 1975 revolution.

The original structures of the European Communities, it should be noted, were far more highly developed and more politically ambitious than those proposed over forty years later in the North American Free Trade Agreement (NAFTA) and the Asia-Pacific Economic Cooperation (APEC) group. The member states of the EC have invested heavily in institutional development over forty years, at some domestic cost but to substantial collective benefit. These structures included central institutions with real autonomy—both political and legal—within defined fields of policy competence. They included a rudimentary central budget, mechanisms for financial transfers, and consultative institutions for democratic and functional representation. They created a system of law which national courts have accepted as directly applicable, in which the European Court of Justice operates as the supreme court and in which private actors have the right to sue national governments. Redress in cases of nonimplementation of Community rules and regulations was thus provided for individuals and companies within the institutional structures established, enforceable through national courts against their own governments.

The EC's institutional structure represents an intricate mixture of federal, functional, and intergovernmental elements. The European Court of Justice and the Community system of law, the European

2. Preamble to the treaty establishing the European Economic Community, signed in Rome on March 25, 1957. As Spain, Portugal, and Greece moved from authoritarian government toward applying for EC membership, the European Parliament, Commission, and Council of Ministers added a Joint Declaration (published in the EC's *Official Journal of the European Community*, vol. 20, no. C 103/1) spelling out to potential applicants that "the treaties establishing the European Communities are based on the principle of respect for the law; . . . as the Court of Justice has recognized, that law comprises, over and above the rules embodied in the Treaties and secondary Community legislation, the general principles of law and in particular the fundamental rights, principles and rights on which the constitutional law of the Member States is based." Neither NAFTA nor APEC has imposed any such conditions for membership, nor would Mexico, Indonesia, or Singapore, let alone the People's Republic of China, satisfy the conditions set.

Parliament (directly elected since 1979, it is the only representative assembly of this sort above the level of the nation-state), and common resources and financial transfers, represent federal elements. The Council of Ministers (a collective entity that meets in different compositions to deal with such issues as external trade, competition, finance, agriculture, and transport) and its extensive substructure of official committees represents the intergovernmental element, with twice-yearly meetings of the heads of government on the European Council providing overall political direction. The European Commission, with its ethos of technocratic and rational administration of distinct areas of policy, represents the functional element: an ethos derived from French administrative traditions and from the liberal-idealist tradition of international relations.[3] The relationship between the Commission and the Council is the core of the Community policymaking process. The "bureaucracy" that outsiders attack consists largely of national officials participating in Commission and Council committees, not of the Commission as an independent entity. The most striking phenomenon of formal European integration has in many ways been the interpenetration of national administrations, with officials and ministers from different governments in close and continuous contact.

There were clear normative undertones in the design of these institutions: beliefs in the superiority of rational administration to irrational nationalism, pressures from idealists for moves away from a Europe of nation-states toward a "European Union."[4] The signatory governments to the treaties spoke not simply of economic advantage but of "the contribution which an organized and vital Europe can make to civilization," of their resolve "to substitute for age-old rivalries the merging of their essential interests," and of their determination "to lay the foundations for institutions which will give direction to a destiny henceforward shared."[5] Underneath this rhetoric, national governments bargained with each other to

3. Webb (1983); Mitrany (1943).

4. The Brussels Treaty was signed by five governments in 1948, revised in 1954, and entered into force in 1955 as the Treaty of Western European Union (WEU). It has long since lost the ambitious tones of its 1955 title. Karl Deutsch remarks that the attraction of the term "union" to those setting out to build a political community is its intrinsic ambiguity: implying federation to some, confederation to others, close alliance among independent states to yet others; see Deutsch and others (1957, p. 11).

5. Preamble to ECSC Treaty, 1951.

promote their national interests. The rhetoric with which politicians phrased their demands, however, significantly affected their definition of national interests and raised awareness of an underlying common purpose.

The structures thus established provided a framework of and for *formal integration:* common institutions, through which to develop rules and policies, to regulate, channel, redirect, encourage, or inhibit economic and social flows. Within this framework, once established, *informal integration* developed: patterns of interaction that flow without further deliberate governmental decisions, following the dynamics of markets, technology, communication networks, and social exchange, or the influence of social, political, or religious movements. Formal integration is by definition a discontinuous process, proceeding treaty by treaty, regulation by regulation, decision by decision. Informal integration (or disintegration) is a matter of flows and exchanges, of the gradual growth (or decay) of networks of interaction. The relationship between these two processes is complex, as West European governments have discovered. The treaties themselves set a secure framework for the rapid development of informal integration, within the wider framework of the "Western" Organization for European Economic Cooperation (later renamed the Organization for Economic Cooperation and Development [OECD]). The flow of informal integration across Western Europe in the 1970s and early 1980s in turn created pressures for further deepening of the formal structures of rules and institutions in order to manage their impact.[6]

The level of development of West European economies in the 1950s was not, however, sufficiently advanced as to require extensive international regulation, reaching deep into the domestic jurisdiction of nation-states. The European Coal and Steel Community set up detailed regimes, with common financing, in highly limited areas, to manage structural adjustment within a widening market. The European Economic Community moved rapidly to develop a highly integrated and *dirigiste* common agricultural regime. But for the most part such measures of *positive integration*—the creation of new regulatory regimes—were unnecessary within a European market charac-

---

6. The definition of "integration" is explored further in the introductory chapter to William Wallace (1991a).

terized by trade among semiautonomous national economies and national companies within these national economies; *negative integration*—the removal of barriers to cross-border trade—was sufficient for the time.[7]

It was the transformation of the West European (and OECD) economy in the 1970s and 1980s—under the impetus of technological, managerial, financial, and social changes—that pushed the EC toward deeper formal integration. The existence of an established set of institutional structures, and the learned experience of working together through these institutional structures over an already extended period, provided the basis on which this deepening of the penetration of regionally negotiated rules into domestic jurisdictions, and the parallel broadening of the agenda of formal integration, was achieved. The gradual expansion of the Community from a small and cohesive core to include a broader and more diverse group of member states, with an associated periphery of nonmember states, maintained a degree of cohesion and direction under changing conditions.

The Community responded to the impact of technological change, and to fears about the obstacles that Western Europe's incompletely integrated markets presented in maintaining industrial competitiveness with Japan and other rising east Asian economies, by moving from a pattern of detailed harmonization of standards and regulations to greater acceptance of mutual recognition of national standards. It also initiated a number of collaborative programs in high technology, in imitation of Japanese precompetitive schemes. Revision of the EC's decision rules in the 1986 Single European Act to allow for greater use of qualified majority voting was accompanied by the launch of the high-profile 1992 Program, designed to accelerate the mixed processes of harmonization and mutual recognition required to move toward a fully integrated single market.

International economic integration may alternatively be defined as the removal of barriers to trade between national economies (shallow integration) and the negotiation of common rules and standards to remove what might otherwise constitute nontarriff barriers to trade within a single market (deep integration). The shift from shallow to deep integration, in Europe as elsewhere, has brought into play a range of broader political issues, from environmental standards to

7. Pinder (1968).

social protection, company law, cross-border crime, the appropriate boundary between the public and the private sectors, and the provision (and financing) of public goods.[8] The disruption that currency fluctuations cause for trade and payments within a single market has led to successive attempts to move toward a single currency: a move that may be economically rational but that also strikes politically close to the heart of sovereignty and national identity. Multilateral bargaining to integrate markets further has led to successive package deals, in which compensation to those most at risk of immediate loss from integration, and financial transfers from the stronger to the weaker economies, have become significant. Such distributive politics has led to gradual growth in the size of the EC budget and to pressures from the less prosperous and peripheral states for further financial transfers.

It has proved extremely difficult to hold the boundaries between economic and political integration, or between policy areas assigned to the Community level and those retained for national governments. Trade issues have raised questions regarding foreign policy principles in relation to Eastern Europe, the Middle East, and South Africa. Competition rules have set the Community authorities against national and local authorities determined to preserve employment (or promote growth) in their own territories. Policing, monetary integration, and redistribution raise central issues for democratic states of accountability and of representation within the EC's opaque process of policymaking. Resistance to the transfer of successive areas of policy to Brussels has led to attempts to reverse this centralizing trend, most recently by incorporating the principle of "subsidiarity" into the Maastricht Treaty on European Union (article 3b). But it has proved impossible to agree on any substantial list of areas to be returned to exclusively national jurisdiction. National governments themselves press new issues onto the Community agenda even as they demand that others be removed; negotiation over the level at which decisions should be made is itself a political process, only partially subject to rational analysis.

8. It should, however, be noted that social policy was included in the original treaties, including such detailed issues as "prevention of occupational accidents and diseases, occupational hygiene, the right of association and collective bargaining between employers and workers . . . , equal pay without discrimination on sex means . . . , [and] equivalence between paid holiday schemes"; see EEC Treaty, articles 118–120.

Regional integration within Western Europe has thus been a highly political process, both promoting economic integration and responding to the impact of economic and technical change. National governments have bargained to maintain as much autonomy as possible while gaining as many benefits from further integration as possible. Out of this pull and push between contradictory imperatives has emerged a pattern of multilevel government, in effect a weak confederation, characterized by a disaggregated and immensely "heavy" policymaking process. The institutional compromise struck between sovereignty and federation has created a system in which the structure and powers of the different institutions are themselves under continuing renegotiation. The attempt by the members of the European Free Trade Association (EFTA) to strike a less institutionally integrated bargain, in the European Economic Area (EEA) agreement—a framework more comparable to NAFTA than to the EC itself—failed, however, to find an alternative formula for managing deep integration which could satisfy their needs. By the time the EEA negotiations had been completed the majority of EFTA states were moving toward applications for full EC membership.

But deepening international integration has appeared to weaken national integration. Resistance to further transfers of authority has arisen, not only in the peripheral states of Western Europe but also within its core countries, as formally agreed-upon legislation strikes at the autonomy and diversity of national and subnational government. Integration of markets, of governments and national administrations, and of business and banking elites has not brought about any comparable integration of national politics or of national publics. National political leaders have found themselves caught between electoral fears of lost autonomy and electoral demands for the economic growth that only further integration can provide. Deep integration has presented a challenge to national identity. Responses have included electoral revolts against established political parties and the reassertion of regional identities against formerly centralized states.

The removal of the international security framework within which West European integration developed has added new complications— forcing a further widening of the regional agenda and raising delicate questions of institutional enlargement and of the limits to regional integration. The role of the United States as external hegemon and security guarantor was a crucial factor in the evolution of the EC. It contained Germany, the potential regional hegemon, giving the French sufficient confidence in their security to build a bilateral relationship with Federal Germany that became a driving force in European integration. It allowed West European governments to avoid questions of West European foreign policy and defense, absorbing these into the Atlantic Alliance under U.S. leadership. It also set clear boundaries to the enlargement of regional institutions. Reconciliation between regional and "Western" global priorities was ensured by mutual recognition on both sides of the Atlantic of the overriding importance of the security relationship, reflected in European willingness to accept American leadership on economic and political issues in return for assurance of security sponsorship.

The end of the cold war has therefore raised a number of awkward questions about the relationship between regional European integration and global economic cooperation—as well as about the structure and extent of the European region. West European states have found it difficult to adjust to the heavier economic, political, and security responsibilities thrust upon them; U.S. administrations have found it difficult to define a more equally balanced relationship. U.S. and West European responses to the transformation of Eastern Europe have differed in emphasis. For Western Europe the determination of former socialist states to "rejoin the West" poses uncomfortable choices about adjustment of established policies, about institutional adaptation to a larger membership, and about the limits to be set on further enlargement.

The experience of deep integration within Western Europe does not therefore provide a model for others to follow. Its historical development was rooted in a stage of economic development and a security framework that have now both disappeared. The institutional structures that West European governments agreed to under those past circumstances have managed to respond to the very different challenges posed by economic and industrial transformation in the 1970s and 1980s. Political, economic, and security motivations have been entangled in the evolution of West European regional integration from the 1940s to the 1990s.

The attempt to create a stable structure for the management of integration that would fall halfway between the sovereign nation-state and a regional federation has led to a heavy and slow-moving pattern of policymaking, in which wider global and political interests risk being squeezed out in the multilateral and multilevel bargaining that characterizes the EC. Enlargement to include both the former European neutral states of EFTA and the former socialist states of central and eastern Europe would complicate internal bargaining and distract attention from the competing priorities of global cooperation. Effective regional integration among advanced economies may well require institutional capacities at least as highly developed as those that the EC has created. Global integration on the basis of such regional groups is, however, likely to falter if regional institutional capabilities are no stronger than this. Preoccupation with multilateral bargaining among states in the region would leave insufficient spare political resources to play a positive role in global economic management within a multipolar world economy.

Chapter 2

The Particularities of the West European Experience

*T*HE development of the structure of West European integration was *not* a response to the problems posed by intense economic interdependence. Its framework was set forty years ago by governments rebuilding their national economies under American leadership after a devastating war. Nor do its underlying rationale and impetus provide a model for other regions of the world. The motivations of its founders were fundamentally political—the containment of a divided Germany—and its driving force has been that of Franco-German reconciliation. The historical context within which West European integration got under way was highly specific, set by the aftermath of war, the presence of a benevolent American hegemon, and a malevolent external Soviet threat. The European Community (EC) was part of the Western cold war system and developed within that system.

The level of economic and technological development within which West European integration was designed was that of the transition from the steam age to the age of electricity and mass production. The European Coal and Steel Community (ECSC) linked together the (then) strategic industries of France and Germany, the foundations for industrial reconstruction in the 1950s. The geographic concentration of the core states of Western Europe, grouped around the Rhine Valley and delta, stretching out from there down the Rhone Valley and across the Alps to the northern Mediterranean and across the narrow waters of the English Channel, is unparalleled elsewhere in the world. Shared cultural reference points, shared history, shared disaster in the war of 1939–45, and shared values emphasized by their American liberators and by the political leaders who emerged out of resistance and defeat all provided the foundations on which they hoped to build a political community.

The EC's response to the transformation of the region's economy in the 1970s and 1980s therefore took place within an already established institutional framework, with its own systems of supranational law and intensive intergovernmental bargaining. Institutions matter. Their decision rules shape and moderate conflict among member governments and alter the balance of influence among them. A European regional system in the 1990s without the firmly entrenched institutions of the European Union (EU) would leave Germany as *the* central player, France struggling to build alliances around Germany, and smaller states like the Netherlands and Belgium without significant influence. The consistency of Dutch and Belgian support for stronger EC/EU institutions reflects the appreciation of those countries that these institutions provide the best means of mitigating their unavoidable dependence on Germany and of transforming bilateral vulnerability into multilateral bargaining. The strength of French support for the EU reflects the same appreciation of long-term national interest—made more acute after 1990 by recognition that its larger and more economically successful German partner was no longer constrained by territorial division and security dependence on its allies, making it even more in French interests to contain German influence within strong multilateral institutions.[1]

The model of deep integration that West European experience offers can therefore be of only limited relevance for other groups of states as they move toward the construction of regional regimes without the benefit of the long (and often painful) learning process through which West European governments worked for several polit-

---

1. The argument advanced by a discussant in the Brookings Institution working conference on this project in January 1994 that "the processes at work in the EC today are, at root, the same ones that we see in the years of negotiation between the USA and Japan . . . or even the kind of talks that we are having with the Chinese about what domestic changes we would demand there in order to maintain trade at particular levels" fundamentally understates both the difference between bilateral and multilateral negotiations and the difference between negotiations within the context of entrenched institutions and negotiations on the basis of classical intergovernmental bargaining. John Mearsheimer's depiction of post–cold war intra-European international relations in classic balance of power terms, widely quoted within the United States, similarly ignored the significance of this intricate network of institutional commitments and transgovernmental links; see Mearsheimer (1990).

ical generations. The stresses created by building a deeply integrated community that goes far beyond traditional assumptions about state sovereignty while stopping well short of federation do nevertheless have lessons to offer. So does the overloaded character of Western Europe's dispersed and intricate policymaking process, in which the preoccupation with striking internal bargains so often distracts attention from external considerations. The West European experience does, therefore, have lessons for others pursuing the intrusive regimes of competition policy, financial regulation, labor market harmonization, environmental regulation, compatible tax regimes, and fiscal transfers that crowd the agenda for regional integration in North America and elsewhere. But those lessons provide little comfort for those who—like the authors of *A Vision for APEC*—seek to create economic communities in other regions without the political imperatives and the deliberate creation of new institutions that set the framework for the integration of Western Europe.[2]

The Historical Context

The context within which the structures of West European regional integration were built was determined by the disaster of World War II and the confrontation between the wartime Soviet and American allies that followed. Scarcely twenty years after the destruction of the Great War of 1914–18, the European state system had erupted into a second general war, which ended with Soviet and American forces meeting in the center of a devastated continent. Economic disorder, recession, and competing protectionist policies had marked the interwar period, as much as disputes over national minorities and territorial claims. For many of those whose wartime experience had been of exile, imprisonment, or clandestine resistance, the nation-state had failed. It had been unable to provide either the security or the prosperity on which its legitimacy as a model for government rested.

The central problem of the European international system since the 1860s had been how to accommodate the unification of Germany—the largest nation within Europe west of semi-Asiatic Russia—without permitting it to exercise regional hegemony. In the nineteenth-century order, with European powers competing for extra-European empire,

2. Asia-Pacific Economic Cooperation (1993).

German and Austrian ambitions to extend their imperium over south-eastern Europe and the Ottoman Empire competed with Russian imperial ambitions and threatened the interests of Britain, France, and Italy. The dynamism of the German economy, its rapid industrialization supported by active state intervention and protection, had made it by 1914 the first trading partner of almost every other continental European state. "Round Germany," John Maynard Keynes noted in arguing unsuccessfully for a generous policy toward Germany in the peace settlement, "the rest of the European economic system grouped itself, and on the prosperity of Germany the prosperity and enterprise of the rest of the Continent mainly depended."[3]

The 1919 settlement had left Germans aggrieved, the European economy unbalanced, insecure new "nation-states" occupying the territories of the former Austrian-Hungarian empire, a politically triumphant but economically weak and multinational Poland, and a half-excluded and professedly revolutionary Russia. The drift toward a second war, for liberal West Europeans, involved much agonizing over competing claims to self-determination in central and Eastern Europe, as the "rights" of German and Hungarian minorities clashed with the security of the states within whose boundaries the Versailles treaties had left them.

The German drive to revise the 1919 settlement carried the Third Reich to a position of regional hegemony that at its peak in 1941—42 was as dominant as that which Napoleonic France had briefly achieved a century and a half before: reincorporating Austria, Bohemia, Alsace-Lorraine, and much of interwar Poland into the German Reich, and occupying the rest of continental Europe as far east as the Ukraine and the western Caucasus. Frontiers were redrawn and populations were relocated, or even enslaved or eliminated, while the Soviet Union, struggling to defend its own multinational state against German attack, also shifted populations on a grand scale. The ultimate defeat of Germany was accompanied by further mass relocation, as millions of displaced persons feared to return home while the victors deported the German minorities whose claims had provided the *casus belli*.

The impetus that led to the creation of formal institutions for the integration of West European states, deliberately designed with supra-

3. Keynes (1919, p. 15).

national characteristics, stemmed from this second European war and from the memories and fears of those who took charge of postwar reconstruction. The United States, which emerged in 1945 as the dominant military and economic power in Western Europe, was led by men conscious of the failures of 1919 and by the dangers of further postwar revolutions—which would attract the political, and perhaps also military, support of the professedly revolutionary Soviet Union. The Marshall Plan marked the beginning of West European economic integration. An American initiative, it provided economic assistance on political conditions and was intended to promote the economic recovery needed to sustain stable democratic government, to push recipient governments into close cooperation, to bolster domestic resistance to communist alternatives, and to underpin the idea that Western Europe—with North America—now formed part of the "West" rather than representing a potential "third force" between the United States and the Soviet Union.[4]

Americans' enthusiasm for a western-oriented European federation stemmed from their own federal history and from their strong perception that disunity among the tightly packed states of Western and central Europe would threaten a repetition of the bitter experience of the interwar years. The Organization for European Economic Cooperation (OEEC), set up on American insistence to administer Marshall Plan assistance, was intended under the guidance of the U.S. Economic Cooperation Administration to promote economic and monetary union among the cooperating European states.[5] Alongside this program substantial American assistance, both overt and covert, was provided for the European Movement and other federalist groups to promote the idea of a politically integrated Western Europe.[6]

American interests interacted with those of the major West European governments. The British had been the most determined to tie

4. Readers should recall that in the late 1940s the second and third largest communist parties, after that of the Soviet Union, were those of France and Italy, and that the role of communists in resistance movements and of the Red Army in liberating occupied Europe had given the communist movement considerable legitimacy across Europe. Even the British government briefly flirted with the idea of a European "third force" in 1946–47, before committing itself to a "Western" alliance. For a discussion of the concept's continuing appeal see Cleveland (1966).

5. Hogan (1987); Ellwood (1992).

6. Aldrich (1994).

the United States into a long-term European commitment in the immediate aftermath of the war, with the Marshall Plan and the OEEC, and the Atlantic Alliance, as the institutions for European-Atlantic cooperation. However, when the British Labour government resisted the transfers of sovereignty to international European institutions that American policymakers sought, American influence was exerted in support of those in France and the low countries who were prepared to take the supranational route. Motivations within the elites of these countries ranged from idealist support for European federation, through recognition that small states could no longer pursue security and prosperity on their own, to fear of a reviving Germany uncontained by a strong multilateral framework. The foundations of the Franco-German relationship which has since the 1950s been the core of the process of European integration, rested upon mutual fear and insecurity, moderated by American political leadership and security guarantees. The French feared an economically and politically resurgent Germany, but recognized that attempts to prevent reconstruction would arouse the same resentments as in the 1920s. The leadership of divided Germany, emerging from its occupation status, feared isolation and sought a framework for recovering autonomy without arousing the hostility of its neighbors.

The outbreak of the Korean War in 1950, occurring under conditions of high tension across Europe, pushed the major actors further toward a supranational approach. American policymakers, already supporting a more rapid restitution of (West) German economic and political autonomy than Germany's immediate neighbors wished, now pressed for the rearmament of Germany to provide the ground forces needed to resist the feared Soviet advance. With the Schuman Plan for a European Coal and Steel Community already under negotiation, a succession of other integrative plans and proposals were floated: for a European Defence Community (EDC)—and a European Political Community to control it; functionally integrated organizations for transport, energy, and agriculture; and, after the collapse of the EDC proposals and their replacement by the looser Western European Union Treaty, for a common market in industry and agriculture and an atomic energy community. These last two took shape as the Treaties of Rome establishing the European Economic Community (EEC) and the European Atomic Energy Community, which entered into force in January 1958.

The peculiar historical circumstances that pushed six European states into accepting so tightly integrated a structure for economic cooperation have now altered beyond recognition. Yet the institutions created under those circumstances remain, firmly embedded after forty years of operation. The desperate need for postwar reconstruction; the instability and vulnerability of governments attempting to reestablish authority over countries occupied during the war; the common dependence on the United States both for economic assistance and for security; the shared perception of an internal and external threat from communism and the Soviet Union; the common preoccupation with the reconstruction of a divided Germany that would not reawaken the nightmares from which European countries had so recently escaped—all these pushed the six founding states of the EC toward accepting mutual limitation of sovereignty. Those states whose experience of World War II had been less desperate— Denmark, occupied but not fought over; occupied but remote Norway; neutral Sweden; and above all unoccupied Britain—did not feel subject to the same imperatives.

There was, of course, a wider institutionalized "Europe" from the earliest postwar years, defined by those states that accepted the offer of Marshall Plan aid and the conditions attached to it, formalized in the closely linked memberships of the OEEC and OECD and the Council of Europe.[7] This was "free" Europe, its eastern boundaries defined by the limits of Soviet military power after 1945. Greece and Turkey, for geopolitical reasons, thus became part of "the West," while Czechoslovakia and Poland became part of the excluded "East." The conditions of membership also defined a certain conception of Europe and of the rules of state interaction, which imposed limits on national sovereignty considerably greater than those within any other regional international organization outside the socialist bloc. Market economies and liberal/constitutional systems were conditions of en-

7. The OEEC was transformed into the Organization for Economic Cooperation and Development (OECD) in 1960; see Urwin (1991). After the first postwar surge of hopeful political activity the Council of Europe evolved into a useful secondary organization focusing on democratic government, educational exchange, and intergovernmental consultations on a wide range of functional issues. Membership is considerably wider than that of the EU; it had risen from twenty-six members in 1989 to thirty-two in 1994. The standards of democratic government and civil liberty that the Council of Europe set as conditions for membership have led former socialist states to see acceptance into this organization as an important step toward satisfying the criteria for EU membership.

try. Spain under Franco remained largely outside the evolving West European regional system, dependent upon bilateral ties with America. Greece and Turkey have both on occasion been temporarily suspended from Council of Europe membership for unacceptable domestic political behavior, with the neutral democracies of Scandinavia prominent alongside EC member governments in enforcing the rules. This was shallower integration, under American sponsorship, with political preconditions—and within a broad United States–protected security community.

The split within the OEEC in 1949–50, between those prepared to pursue supranational integration and those determined to limit cooperation to intergovernmental negotiation, did not prevent progressive economic integration across the entire OEEC area. The EEC itself after its initiation in 1958 moved rapidly to sign association agreements with Greece and Turkey, in the early 1960s. All the member states of the looser European Free Trade Association (EFTA) (established by the Stockholm Convention of 1960, in response to the Treaties of Rome) negotiated bilateral agreements with the EEC in the years that followed. Britain and Denmark moved from EFTA to EC membership in 1973, together with Ireland (a non-EFTA member that had until then relied on bilateral association with Britain); Norway failed to join them only when the terms of EC entry were rejected in a national referendum. Full EC membership for Greece (in 1981) and Spain and Portugal (in 1986) was seen by both sides as a reward for their transition to democracy and as a means of consolidating democracy. Economic access and financial transfers were thus granted for political reasons.

Those states that for historical and political reasons were still reluctant to accept the logic of full EC membership responded in the 1980s to economic and industrial transformation by seeking to add to the EC/EFTA relationship the closest possible association with the EC short of full membership. Between 1989 and 1992 the two groups negotiated a multilateral agreement to establish a European Economic Area, which—the EFTA governments hoped—would give them a degree of direct access to Community decisionmaking.[8] Their reluctance to accept the implications of full membership reflected their perception that the EC was, with the North Atlantic Treaty

8. Helen Wallace (1991b).

Organization (NATO), intrinsically part of the American-led western security system. This was a perception shared by the newly democratic Spanish government in the late 1970s, which moved to join NATO and the EC self-consciously in parallel.

West European integration was thus first and foremost a political enterprise, harnessing economic means to political objectives. The signatory governments to the Treaty of Paris in April 1951, which established the supranational ECSC, declared in the preamble that they were "Resolved to substitute for age-old rivalries the merging of their essential interests; to create, by establishing an economic community, the basis for a broader and deeper community among peoples long divided by bloody conflicts; and to lay the foundations for institutions which will give direction to a destiny henceforward shared."[9]

The Importance of Geography: The Reintegration of Charlemagne's Europe

The peculiar circumstances of postwar divided Europe also set clear geographical limits on the region to be integrated. Soviet occupation cut off east-central Europe, including all the eastern territories of imperial Germany. The east-west frontier marked a boundary between "West" and "East" remarkably similar to that which had marked the boundary between Germans and Slavs a thousand years before. Indeed, as enthusiasts for "European union" pointed out, the territory of the EC Six corresponded closely to that of the Western Empire reestablished by Charlemagne in A.D. 800, with the Rhine Valley and delta as its core, stretching across Burgundy, southern Germany, and the Alpine passes to northern Italy, with southwestern France and the north German plain as its outer limits.[10]

A territory compact enough to be ruled under ninth-century conditions from Aachen did not present insuperable obstacles to twentieth-century integration. State- and nation-building in the eighteenth and nineteenth centuries had cut across its long-established commu-

9. Preamble to the ECSC Treaty, 1951.

10. See, for example, Lord Gladwyn (1966). Southern Italy was outside Charlemagne's kingdom—still part of the Byzantine empire in the ninth century—and present-day Switzerland, Austria, and Slovenia were inside. See also William Wallace (1990, chapter 2).

nication and trade routes, imposing border controls and redirecting travel and trade through national capitals. The Netherlands had been carved out of the Holy Roman Empire in the sixteenth century through rebellion against the Hapsburgs. Belgium and Luxembourg were artificial states created out of the Spanish Hapsburgs' remaining "low German" possessions and the Dutch failure to hold them together after 1815 as a single state.

Northern Italy had been politically and economically linked to southern Italy through unification only seventy years before World War II, after centuries of close contact with the German world and with France. The Rhineland had come under Prussian control in 1815, but Catholic and urban Rhinelanders like Konrad Adenauer retained a strong sense of separateness from Protestant Berlin and agricultural Prussia. The establishment of the Federal Republic's capital in Bonn underlined the shift of balance in this new and smaller Germany south and west. It was practical to travel by train between all of the capitals of the Six except Rome within a few hours. Milan, Italy's second city and financial and commercial capital, had the advantage over Rome that it was much better positioned in this network of railways and personal contacts.[11]

Regular contacts among elites inside and around government were therefore possible from the outset, and they were of an intensity that only became practical in other international regions with the advent of mass air travel. Businessmen, bankers, officials, politicians, trade union leaders, journalists, and intellectuals developed transnational networks as close as those that had held together European royalty and aristocracy in the years before World War I.[12] The early development of parliamentary "assemblies"—for the Council of Europe, for the ECSC, and for the West European Union—composed of members of national parliaments able to gather for regular meetings without losing touch with their domestic base, depended upon this combination of short distances and good surface communications.

Western Europe's concentration of territory, population, economic activity, and social interaction was thus—and remains—a vital aspect

11. American readers puzzled by the siting of the Bank for International Settlements in Basel should refer to old railway maps of Europe. Basel, with French, German, and Swiss railway stations, was a prime railway junction in the heart of industrialized Europe—and thus a convenient point at which central bankers could gather.

12. Tuchman (1966) describes this intense international aristocratic society, traveling by ship and railway from spa to spa and palace to palace.

of the region's progress in formal and informal integration. The entire territory of the original six countries could be contained within the fifteen northeastern states of the United States. The distance from Brussels to Rome is similar to that between Boston and Chicago; Brussels-Paris and Brussels-London are comparable to Boston–New York, and Brussels-Bonn and Brussels–the Hague are comparable to New York–Washington. France alone counted for half of the area of the Six; if southern Italy is understood to have been politically and economically peripheral to this interstate region, its density and compactness become even more clear.

Improvement of internal communications in the 1960s, 1970s, and 1980s brought these states and their elites even closer together. Hans-Dietrich Genscher, German foreign minister from 1974 to 1991, habitually traveled between Bonn, Brussels, and the Hague by car, and sometimes also between Bonn and Paris, talking continuously on his car phone as he traveled. Motorways extended across national frontiers; state rail authorities cooperated to build a trans-European intercity network, with improvements in the 1990s set to bring Paris, Brussels, Cologne and Bonn, Amsterdam and the Hague, and (through the Channel Tunnel) London still closer through "trains à grande vitesse."

Successive rounds of enlargement, in 1973, 1981, and 1986, expanded the EC's geographic spread. Comparisons between this much-enlarged entity and the United States nevertheless remain instructive. The population of the current twelve-member EC is approximately 140 percent of that of the United States but occupies a territory only a quarter the size. All members except Britain and Ireland to the west and Greece to the east share the same time zone. From London six other capitals are accessible within an hour's flying time, and a further four within two to two and a half hours; only Athens, four and a half hours away, remains an outlier. The normal working practices of national ministers, senior officials, the informal policy community, businessmen, and bankers from the 1970s on have included regular visits to each other's capitals, out and back in a single day; many senior policymakers travel several times each week, from intergovernmental committees to bilateral consultations to Community bargaining.[13] Those with private planes—heads of government, ministers,

---

13. Douglas Hurd, the British foreign secretary, remarked at a public meeting with his French counterpart in Paris in 1991 that this was the tenth time they had met in two weeks, and the sixth country in which they had done so.

chief executives—fly over for afternoon meetings or even for dinner, making bilateral consultations an easy and therefore a frequent occurrence.[14] The collective committee style that characterizes European policymaking depends upon the ease with which those who are responsible for formulating and administering national policies are able themselves to participate in multilateral bargaining.

Geographic concentration plus improving communications eased the integration of national economies into a regional economy and in turn created pressures for further integration of regulations and regimes. Once transborder motorway links had been built and direct-dial international telephone links established, it made more sense for major manufacturers to produce and market on a European rather than a nation-by-nation basis. As they attempted to do so, the obstacles presented by separate national regulations became more and more burdensome: lengthy delays to trucks moving parts from plant to plant, on journeys that, without border controls, could take them across two or three national borders in a single day's driving; different national tax regimes, which necessitated detailed paperwork and checks on fuel and goods at each frontier; different regulations on axle weights, truck safety, vehicle exhaust emissions, and hours permitted behind the wheel. The frustrations of the increasing number of international haulage companies and independent truck drivers exploded in a blockade of France's frontiers during the winter of 1984–85: action by private entrepreneurs to force governments to move from national to Community-wide regulations.[15] European industrialists in the early 1980s similarly joined forces with the EC Commission to lobby national governments to abandon national regulations that had presented only minor difficulties to the trade among national economies that had characterized the Western Europe of the 1960s, but had become major obstacles to the integrated production patterns toward which they were moving.[16] The European Round Table of Industrialists had become convinced that the fragmentation of a market that they were learning to think of as a regional economy hampered their ability to compete with their American and Japanese rivals and so

14. It was characteristic of British Prime Minister Margaret Thatcher that she refused to travel to Rome for bilateral British-Italian summits; she strongly preferred to travel out and back in the same day for such meetings and considered Milan to be the outer limit for such expeditions.

15. Pelkmans, Winters, and Wallace (1988, p. 29).

16. Sandholtz and Zysman (1989).

generated powerful support for faster progress toward common standards, and mutual recognition of national standards, to help produce the package of measures that became the 1992 Program.

Improved mass communications and increasing affluence also made for an explosion of cross-border travel, for pleasure, work and study, from the 1960s on. The governments that negotiated the treaty establishing the EEC had been initially reluctant to open their internal borders to labor migration and cross-border patterns of work—fearing a massive transfer of labour from southern Italy to the richer northern countries.[17] Rapid growth in demand for labor in the 1960s, however, drew in migrants not only from southern Italy but also from Portugal, Spain, Yugoslavia, Greece, and Turkey. The rise of mass tourism exerted pressures on border controls as weighty as those presented by rising freight traffic. The annual number of journeys across the English Channel increased by a factor of eight between 1968 and 1988 (from five to forty million a year each way). Summer migrations by the late 1980s represented mass international movement on an unprecedented scale. A third of the population of the Netherlands is believed to leave the country on the first weekend in August, as their main holiday season starts. Almost a million Moroccans travel home across Spain each summer from their workplaces in France and Belgium. Urbanization in France had left room for over a million Belgians, Dutch, Germans, Swiss, and British to buy second homes in French villages, leaving some rural areas with a majority of affluent foreigners as homeowners. Mass summer migrations to the Mediterranean are supplemented by winter migrations to the Alps (and, by the wealthy elderly, from the cold north to the winter sun of the south, in a pattern that European air traffic controllers have compared to U.S. east coast summer and winter flows between New York and New England and Florida).[18]

Affluent West Europeans had thus come by the 1980s to regard the western half of the continent, rather than their own national boundaries, as their relevant social space. Presentation of passports and submission to customs checks at EC internal borders had given way to cursory glances at identity cards, with passports no longer required for intra-EC travel. New policy issues pushed onto the Community agenda—and onto the agenda of the wider Council of Europe—re-

17. Romero (1993).
18. Romero (1991).

flected this trampling across the former boundaries between domestic regulation and international politics. Ownership of second homes by citizens of other West European states had become a sensitive issue in Danish politics and in negotiations between Austria, Switzerland, Norway, and Sweden and the Community. Cooperation among police and intelligence services against drug traffic, terrorism, financial fraud, and other forms of cross-border crime had begun in the early 1970s. It had grown in intensity in the 1980s to include extensive exchanges of sensitive information, a European office of Interpol to handle the rising traffic, and, in 1991, regularization of the intensive contacts that had grown up through their incorporation into the Maastricht Treaty on European Union.[19]

American soldiers driving across Belgium and Luxembourg in the campaign of 1944–45 had remarked upon the absurdity of these little countries claiming separate sovereignties.[20] Forty years later, with communication links across their borders as close as those among Massachusetts, Connecticut, and Rhode Island, these governments themselves and their neighbors were struggling to come to terms with that absurdity. The three Benelux countries had already moved toward removal of most internal border controls in the 1970s. France and Germany agreed bilaterally to abolish border controls between them in 1984. Faced with resistance from Britain in particular to implementation of the formal commitment within the 1987 Single European Act to abolition of controls on internal borders throughout the Community, these five countries then negotiated the Schengen Agreement of 1988, to replace their internal border controls by common rules on external borders, entry requirements, and internal policing.

This step, however, penetrated close to the heart of traditional domestic sovereignty, with distinctive (and not always compatible) traditions of policing and civil order. Pressures in these countries to ease personal travel among their citizens thus came up against resistance to change in politically sensitive areas and against fears of rising cross-border crime and immigration. Implementation was made more difficult by acceptance of Spain and Italy into membership, with their extensive maritime borders looking across the Mediterranean to the

19. Den Boer and Walker (1993)
20. The comment was also made in one of the best "late" films on World War II, *The Americanization of Emily,* by James Coburn to Julie Andrews.

rising populations of North Africa. In 1994 the implementing convention for the Schengen Agreement had therefore still not come into force.

The contradictory stance in which opposing political and social pressures left governments was reflected in the inclusion in the Maastricht Treaty on European Union of Title VI, covering "Provisions on cooperation in the fields of justice and home affairs." This reiterated the goals of "free movement of persons," and common "rules governing the crossing by persons of the external borders of the Member States" (article K.1) and brought the extensive network of intergovernmental consultations that had developed since the 1970s among police, intelligence services, and interior ministries within the formal framework of the treaty. But title VI was reticent about moves toward full implementation of the goal of free movement.[21]

Cultural Community as a Basis for Political Integration

Europe in 1500, before the political-religious conflicts that divided Western Christendom and led (in the Westphalia Settlement a century and a half later) to the establishment of a system of states, was almost as much a political and cultural community as China, with an emperor whose authority was weak outside his personal domains and a shared sacred language and religion, with the regular clergy of the Catholic church providing some of the same functions as the mandarin class. The rise first of the modern state and then of the ideology of nationalism split this former community of Western Christendom into nation-states. These consolidated in the nineteenth and early twentieth centuries into competing alliance systems with bitter conflicts over territory, markets, and prestige and competing ideologies of national superiority. Europe's expansion across the globe, and its apparently absolute supremacy over other cultures and civilizations, allowed its major powers to compete on a global stage, on which conflict among European states was moderated only by their collective assumption of the shared superiority of European values over those of all non-European nations.

The double disaster of the two world wars, and the deep shocks to easy assumptions about European superiority presented by Nazism

21. Anderson and den Boer (1994).

and Stalinism, brought memories and myths of Europe as a cultural community back to prominence in postwar Western Europe. Identification of "Europe" with a common history and cultural tradition was made easier by the postwar shrinking of the European core to the six largely Catholic countries that formed the original ECSC, including a divided Germany that had lost much of its Protestant north and a Netherlands dependent on a carefully constructed domestic balance among Protestants, Catholics, and secular Liberals and Socialists. Christian democratic leaders—Adenauer, de Gasperi, Schuman—and their parties, sharing a common political perspective and a common set of ideological assumptions, played a central role in shaping the structure of the ECSC and EEC.

Close links among Social Democrats and Liberals, forged into party internationals out of common exile or resistance contacts in the passionately heated atmosphere of the immediate postwar years, also brought the elites and assumptions of separate sets of national policymakers together. American promotion of "Western" values, and "Western" civilization, against the challenge of "Eastern" state socialism also underlined Western Europe's shared history and culture; American financial subsidies assisted social democratic parties against communist parties, European federalists against defenders of national differences. But it was the Catholic Christian Democrat tradition that placed its particular stamp on the development of formal West European integration, with its doctrines of "social capitalism" and social markets—of a partnership between the state and the corporate representatives of industry and labor to promote the general interest. Protestants and liberals in Germany and the Netherlands entertained severe doubts about the priorities their colleagues and their partners pursued. They were less happy about pushing ahead toward closer integration among the Six without waiting for the (liberal and Protestant) British and Scandinavians to follow, and about accepting degrees of state intervention and market guidance beyond the accepted bounds of Keynesian orthodoxy.[22]

This reemphasized common heritage counterbalanced—but did not outweigh—continuing awareness of national differences and bit-

22. I am relying here in particular on Bernard Bouwman's Oxford D.Phil. thesis, "The British Dimension in Dutch European Policy, 1950–1962," 1994. The Protestant Dutch prime minister's doubts in 1956 about French and German plans for further economic integration among the Six, he notes, were sharpened by a remark addressed to him by an Italian minister's wife over dinner during a working visit to Rome: "Isn't it wonderful that our united Europe is going to be a Catholic one?"

ter memories of war, occupation, even atrocity and counter-atrocity. The idea of "Europe," of a common corpus of European values and a common history of European civilization, remained a contested area in the postwar period—and it is still so forty years later.[23] Fear of an independent and economically reconstructed Germany among its neighbors, and the determination of German (and Italian) political leaders to overcome those suspicions and demonstrate their democratic and "European" credentials, were important underlying motivations in pushing the Six toward accepting limitations on their separate national sovereignties. Shared fears of communism, both of internal subversion and of external threat, were an additional negative motivation for integration. Nevertheless the existence of common histories provided a rhetoric, a set of symbols and a shared frame of reference that eased the process of reconciliation between Federal Germany and its neighbors and provided a degree of legitimacy for the transfers of sovereignty that formal integration involved. The Franco-German military parade in Rheims in the spring of 1963, a symbolic event orchestrated to celebrate the bilateral Elysée Treaty, illustrates both the effort that had to be undertaken to reshape national perceptions and the availability of common reference points that political leaders could use: French and German forces parading together outside one of the great gothic cathedrals, whose architectural style stretches across France and into Germany.[24]

The Modern (and Postmodern?) West European State

The contemporary international state system is built upon a West European model. Britain and France were the archetypical state-nations that Germany and Italy strove to imitate, with the new states of eastern and southeastern Europe, Turkey, and Japan following in their path. The states of Western Europe forced through the painful processes of *national* integration during the nineteenth century, assim-

23. Weidenfeld (1984); Rijksbaron and others (1987).

24. The immense and repeated symbolic gestures of reconciliation between previously hostile states that have marked Franco-German relations over the past thirty years have helped to provide a political underpinning to an often tense economic partnership. Successful development of Asian-Pacific Economic Cooperation would be assisted by a similar political investment between Japan and Korea and between Japan and China, sustained over a generation or more.

ilating minorities and creating strong state administrations around metropolitan centers, with national communications radiating out from each capital. High levels of national integration did not, however, prevent serious domestic divisions in the interwar years, which contributed to the drift into a second European (and world) war. The governments that set out to rebuild their nation-states after 1945 were acutely aware of their security weaknesses and of the unavoidability of accepting a degree of economic interdependence if they were to rebuild national prosperity. "What we shall have to combine," Paul-Henri Spaak, as foreign minister of the Belgian government-in-exile, declared in 1941, "is a certain reawakening of nationalism and an indispensable internationalism."[25]

Economic integration, American assistance, and military alliance were preconditions for the reconstruction of national prosperity, and thus of national legitimacy, after 1945. The "thirty glorious years" of sustained economic growth provided steady employment and previously unimagined prosperity for the citizens of West European states, allowed for a substantial shift from rural to urban society in southern France and Italy, and supplied West European governments with the rising revenues needed to broaden their welfare systems, pay for a modernization of infrastructure, and underwrite national industrial and technological development. One of the central paradoxes of the early years of West European integration is that it enabled member governments to reestablish the legitimacy and autonomy of their own state structures.[26] The intergovernmental bargaining that led to the Treaties of Paris and Rome, and that continued to characterize the policymaking process within the European Communities thereafter, represented a series of hard-fought compromises between the maintenance of sovereignty and the transfer of limited powers to formal integrated bodies. President Charles de Gaulle was the most self-conscious about the compromises involved: accepting the necessity of an integrated economic community, but seeking to set sharp limits to its authority; attempting to harness German resources to French ends, but having to harness them through an intensive network of intergovernmental consultations that in turn constrained French freedom of maneuver.

Postwar reconstruction, rebuilding national roads and railways, domestic agriculture, and national industries for arms supply and

25. Quoted in Milward (1992, p. 320).
26. Milward (1992).

export made for only modest incursions into national autonomy. From the early 1960s onward, however, the reconciliation of national autonomy with extensive interdependence and limited supranational authority became steadily more difficult. The cost of subsidizing advanced civil and military technology forced France, Britain, and Germany into bilateral and multilateral collaborative programs, beginning in 1961. Slower growth in the 1970s, combined with a changing demographic balance among their populations, opened up a widening gap between revenues and expenditures and gave rise to fears of "overloaded government" and a "crisis of the welfare state." The electronic revolution, with its immense impact on European (and global) financial markets as well as upon the integration of Europe's manufacturing and service industries, forced national governments into continuous consultations in new fields, fields that had previously been considered to fall within the realm of domestic policy. Industrial adjustment, from mass production and heavy industry to new electronic industries, niche products and specialist services, ate further into national autonomy.[27]

Western Europe as a regional system by the 1980s thus contained within itself an underlying contradiction between the nation-state basis for policymaking and accountability and the increasing incapacity of nation-states, mitigated by high levels of social and economic interaction among West European states and by the evolution of the formal and semiformal institutions through which its governments collaborated. Over the forty years since 1945 its nation-states had relinquished control over some of the central areas of national sovereignty, as European state theorists had understood it, and moved toward collaborative management of other central areas. The power to tax, the management of the national currency, the redistribution of revenue and expenditure, regulation of the economy, industry and agriculture, foreign policy, defense, control over national territorial boundaries, domestic policing, law and citizenship—all have been constrained. All were further limited by the Maastricht Treaty on European Union of 1992. The observer might depict the resulting regional system as consisting of postmodern states, which have moved on from traditional state functions of defense and territorial protection to more limited preoccupations with the partly collaborative, partly competitive pursuit of prosperity and welfare.

27. William Wallace (1994).

Economic and technological logic has swept away much of the traditional rationale for state autonomy within this densely packed international region. Yet the nation-state remains, throughout Europe, the primary focus for political activity and democratic accountability; political logic still starts from the nineteenth-century model of the self-governing national community. The tensions between economic and political logic that have resulted from this divergence provide the key to understanding the ebb and flow of West European international politics, between the defense of sovereignty and the acceptance of further transfers of authority, over the past quarter century.

Chapter 3

The West European Model

*T*HOSE in North America who saw the European Community (EC) at the end of the 1980s as a model for dealing with some of the complexities that deep integration represents underestimated the complexity—and the penetration into domestic sovereignties—of the legal and institutional structures that the EC had established over the preceding thirty years, providing the foundations on which the 1992 Program could be built.[1] The EC is much more than a collection of intensive intergovernmental regimes. It is a mistake of category to compare the EC with the North American Free Trade Agreement (NAFTA), let alone with Asia-Pacific Economic Cooperation (APEC).[2]

The appropriate comparisons for NAFTA are the European Economic Area (EEA) agreement of 1992 between the EC and the European Free Trade Area (EFTA) member states, and the Europe Agreements negotiated in 1992–93 with the former socialist countries of east-central Europe. In contrast to the political commitment of the EC—and the explicitly dynamic and cumulative nature of the process of formal integration that it involved—the EEA was intended to be limited both in terms of potential further development and in terms of political engagement. The Europe Agreements were ambiguous in this regard. Their ex-socialist signatories wished them to be accepted as an intermediate agreement in a process of transition that would

1. Aaron and others (1992).
2. The Eminent Persons Group report to APEC Ministers emphasizes that "there is at present only one real economic bloc: the EC" (p. 16) but goes on to draw parallels in several places between what the EC has achieved and what APEC may wish to develop; see Asia-Pacific Economic Cooperation (1993).

carry them into full membership in the EC, although many within the EC preferred to see them as limited commitments that provided for association without the promise of early or full membership. The failure of the EEA to provide a shallower alternative to the deep integration provided by the EC that could satisfy the governments of the EFTA countries is a significant development for those who look to European experience to provide lessons for other experiments in regional integration, and it is therefore discussed in more detail in the final section of this chapter.

The EC is better understood in its style of operation (and in its built-in weaknesses) in comparison to Canada: a continuous process of multilevel and multi-issue bargaining within a framework of widely agreed-upon and observed rules in which, however, underlying assumptions about the basis for community are not entirely shared. The EC is more confederal in composition than Canada in two important respects: the absence of any centrally directed and funded foreign policy or defense capacity and the lower levels of financial transfers between different member states. The "civilian power" status of the EC rested—until the collapse of the Soviet Union—upon the willingness of the United States to provide an Atlantic framework for collective security and upon the intense sensitivity of the issue of returning to Federal Germany the level of influence over strategic and military questions that would have accrued to Bonn in any autonomous European security structure. The provision of this central function of government—the core of the federative powers with which the executive arm of the government of the United States was provided in the constitution of 1787—by an external power, within a broader Atlantic framework, served to obscure the otherwise deep incursions into the heart of state sovereignty which Community policies had made after thirty years of formal and informal integration.[3]

The institutional framework of the European Communities was established to cope with the political dilemmas of West European cooperation after World War II and the economic challenges of an earlier industrial age. The impetus was fundamentally political: driven by security concerns, by American pressure, and by recognition in France and the low countries that the recovery of the German econ-

3. It should, however, be noted that Canada was never capable of ensuring its own defense. It passed from dependence on British protection to dependence on American, its sovereignty and unity in this respect maintained by outsiders.

omy—to regain its previously pivotal role in European economic development—could only be contained by the creation of an institutional framework for regional integration. The confederal structures that supported the surge of new policies in the 1980s—the degree of autonomy granted to the Commission, the establishment of a Community system of law which overrode national legislation, the principle of common financing of common policies, the introduction of elements of democratic representation and accountability, the provision for decisionmaking by weighted majority—had been established some thirty years earlier in the original treaties and had developed and extended over the intervening years.

The European Community as a Confederal System

The European Coal and Steel Community (ECSC) established under the Treaty of Paris in 1951 was self-consciously supranational, and in some respects self-consciously nonpolitical. It drew upon the experience and ethos both of the administration of occupied Germany and of the French Commissariat du Plan. The model was one of enlightened technocracy: of *fonctionnaires* seeking rational solutions to economic problems and educating those whose cooperation they needed to understand how their interests were best served by common policies through extensive consultation and careful accumulation of information. The confident self-image of the High Authority (and of the two Commissions in their early years) was of an elite technocratic body. Its officials saw themselves as standing apart from the long-established assumptions of national administrations and from the parochial issues of partisan national politics, able therefore to discern the common European interest and to lead national officials, ministers, and interest group representatives in following it.

The institutional structure of the ECSC was partly functional, partly federal, and partly intergovernmental. The High Authority represented the supranational functional element: a collegiate body, drawn from each of the member states but required to be "completely independent in the performance of their duties," while "in the performance of these duties they shall neither take instructions from any Government or from any other body." The prestige of those appointed to the High Authority, and a few years later to the parallel commissions of the European Economic Community (EEC) and the European Atomic Energy Community (Euratom), underpinned this independence of advice and action within the spheres of policy competence granted under the treaties.[4]

The freedom and functions granted to the first High Authority were greater than those that the Treaties of Rome had allowed to the two commissions. Six more years of peace and economic recovery had made national governments more self-confident and more resistant to the transfer of policy competences to other bodies. The functions to be transferred were, moreover, closer to their central concerns—though not yet seen as matters of vital national interest. President Charles de Gaulle, in setting limits on the EEC's ambitions, distinguished between the "low politics" of economic and commercial transactions which it was acceptable to manage collectively through such institutions, and the "high politics" of foreign policy and defense, which must remain firmly within the bounds of sovereign states.

From the outset, it should be emphasized, the High Authority and the Commissions were far more than an international secretariat.[5] Its collegiate status, with one member from each of the smaller states, carried echoes of symbolic representation; the personal status of its members gave it the quality of a "wise men's group," and the capacity to deal with national ministers on equal terms. The officials who filled its supporting services assumed (and were largely granted) a degree of authority in their dealings with national officials and interest group representatives much greater than that possessed by officials of any global international organization. They represented the European interest and campaigned on its behalf while promoting policies to further it and administering those policies already agreed to.

4. The quotations are from article 9 of the ECSC Treaty of Paris, 1951. The High Authority and the commissions of the EEC and Euratom were merged into one in 1967, under the provisions of the 1965 (Merger) treaty establishing a Single Council and Single Commission of the European Communities.

5. The APEC Eminent Persons Group comparison between the Secretariat of the Organization for Economic Cooperation and Development (OECD) and the EC Commission is also a category mistake. The OECD Secretariat works without publicity and without executive functions, servicing intergovernmental committees and producing well-researched (and little noticed) reports. It is certainly not "an embracing bureaucracy" and may very well provide an excellent model for the more modest objectives that APEC has set for itself. The implication in this report that APEC could somehow manage to operate effectively without a secretariat at least as extensive as that which the OECD provides suggests a failure to grasp the full information and agenda-setting requirements of any moves toward deeper integration; see Asia-Pacific Economic Cooperation (1993, p. 57).

A secondary functional aspect was the inclusion in the ECSC of a Consultative Committee, to be "attached to the High Authority" though "appointed by the Council," which consisted of members of "representative organisations," most importantly of organizations representing "producers and workers." Corporate bodies representing functional interests were seen as necessary and legitimate partners for the High Authority and as natural allies in developing common policies. Enthusiasts for functional integration saw this alliance as leading through growing recognition of the superiority of common interests over particular interests to a transfer of loyalties from the national to the Community level.[6] The inclusion of a more widely representative Economic and Social Committee (Ecosoc) in the EEC treaty reflected the same functional and corporatist assumptions about the role of social organizations. Although Ecosoc has failed to achieve the influence and prestige for which its founders hoped, let alone to act as a conduit for the transfer of loyalties, the principle that the Commission should consult on all issues with interested organizations has sunk deeply into the working style of the Community—with implications, which will be explored further later in this chapter, for the entrenchment of established interests and the effective capture of regulatory authorities by those they are supposed to regulate.

The Council of Ministers represented the intergovernmental dimension. The relationship between a supranational High Authority, with the sole right to make proposals to the Council, and the Council itself, with the power of decision, was the core of the policymaking process, with national and supranational elements in deliberate tension. Ministers from each of the member governments were to act within the Council as representatives of their states. They met under rotating national chairmanship, with a small Brussels-based secretariat to service their meetings and liaise with the High Authority and the Commissions. The power of initiative invested in the High Authority and the Commissions, however, gave it a central role in setting the Council's agenda: it was intended to ensure that proposals did not represent the lowest common denominator of intergovernmental compromise, but rather the highest common multiple of the underlying interests of the Community.

As the volume of business grew, the Council spawned subordinate committees to prepare its decisions and to consider Commission

6. Haas (1958). The quotations are from article 18 of the ECSC Treaty.

proposals. As the EEC moved to develop common policies in different functional areas, the Council began to meet in an increasing number of forms: ministers of agriculture, of transport, of finance, and of health, each subset with its own preparatory committees and groups. Once decisions had been made, the tiny staff of the Commission depended upon the cooperation of national administrations to implement them. This requirement called into operation another set of management committees and Commission-led groups and gave the Brussels policy process the character of a spreading network of committees through which the Commission interacted with officials traveling out from national capitals or based in the member states' expanding permanent representations.

Council decisions were to be made partly on the basis of unanimity, partly on the basis of weighted and qualified majority voting. The enormous disparity in the original Six between Luxembourg (with a population of about 350,000) and France, Germany, and Italy (with populations of over 50 million) made it unacceptable to proceed entirely on the basis of sovereign equality where real economic interests were concerned. As in the Federal German constitution, different member states were allocated weighted votes that partially reflected their differences in size—although with a similar bias in favor of the smaller members against the larger.[7] Decisions then required a qualified majority calculated to ensure that the votes of at least two of the three largest states were required for a proposal to be accepted.[8]

This was to be the exercise of collective sovereignty, not simply multilateral bargaining among sovereign states that retained whenever needed the right of unilateral veto. De Gaulle's recognition of the federalizing implications of such a decision process—within which an activist Commission could seek alliances with different coalitions to create majorities for package deals on policy—led to a succession of confrontations with the Commission and its first president, Walter Hallstein, a German law professor and official with a strong commitment to the belief that rational administration was displacing partisan politics.[9] Hallstein's attempt in 1965 to link proposals for the financ-

7. The electoral college for U.S. presidential elections is constructed on similar principles.

8. The original ECSC treaty also qualified the majority required according to proportions of the total coal and steel output of the Community.

9. Hallstein (1973).

ing of the Common Agricultural Policy (CAP) with an increase in the Commission's authority over the raising and spending of EC revenues provoked the "empty chair" crisis, in which the French government suspended its participation in Council meetings and committees. The resulting Luxembourg Compromise of January 1966 substantially undermined the principle of majority voting, recording that "the French delegation considers that, when very important interests are at stake, discussion must be continued until unanimous agreement is reached."[10]

Throughout the decade that followed it remained more common for decisions to be made by consensus than by vote, in spite of the lengthy delays and consultations that such a process involved. But the pressures of increased Community business and the enlargement of the Community from six to nine (then ten, then twelve) made majority voting on less contentious matters a convenient procedure. The willingness of the other nine members to override the British government on the issue of the 1982 agricultural price settlement, declaring that British opposition to the proposals could not be said to constitute a matter of vital national interest sufficient to justify a veto, marked a clear limitation of the scope of the Luxembourg Compromise. The scope of majority voting was extended further under the 1987 Single European Act, and further again under the 1992 Treaty on European Union. It remains the case, however, that member governments are reluctant to override the opposition of any one government when they recognize that its claim that the issue at stake *does* affect vital national interests is rooted in the imperatives of domestic political survival or popular perception.[11]

Creation of a European Council of heads of government (and, in the French case, of state) in 1974, was intended by its French proposers to strengthen the intergovernmental dimension of Community policymaking by bringing back together within a single overall conference the many different negotiations under way in the dispersed network of functional Councils and subordinate committees. The

10. Communiqué from the special meeting of EEC Council of Ministers, Luxembourg, 28–29 January 1966 (reprinted in *Agence Europe*, Brussels, January 30, 1966).

11. The position of the Greek government on the recognition of the "Former Yugoslav Republic of Macedonia" in 1993–94 was a good example of such an interest. Most other member governments were profoundly irritated at the Greek stance, more strongly so when it extended to imposition of unilateral interruption of cross-border trade in defiance of Community law. But they recognized that Greek national identity was seen to be involved and that national passions were running high; recognition was thus delayed by some months, and other governments held back from explicitly outvoting their Greek partner on the issue.

drama—the symbolic and real confrontations—of meetings of the European Council, reported to the attending journalists and television crews by each participating leader and each government spokesman, has immensely increased the visibility of Community policymaking to national publics, at the cost of portraying it most often as a succession of zero-sum games. But the regular and direct involvement of heads of government, meeting two to three times a year, in Community bargaining has at the same time strengthened the collective character of EC policymaking, with prime ministers (and the French president) moving from multilateral meetings to bilateral consultations and back, their diaries devoted increasingly to Community as opposed to domestic business or traditional diplomacy.

The most important federal element in the original treaties was the establishment of a system of Community law, with a European Court of Justice (ECJ) to "ensure that in the interpretation and application of this Treaty, and of rules laid down for the implementation thereof, the law is observed." The evolution of Community law has been one of the most distinctive characteristics of EC policymaking, sharply distinguishing it from traditional international organizations and intergovernmental regimes.[12]

As after 1787 the American Supreme Court had done, the ECJ moved fairly rapidly to assert its supremacy over state law , declaring in the landmark *Costa* v. *ENEL* case of 1964 that "the Member States have limited their sovereign rights, albeit within limited fields, and have thus created a body of law which binds both their individuals and themselves."[13] Community decisions embodied as regulations constitute Community legislation, directly applicable throughout the EC without the need for further national measures. In case of non-implementation, individuals have long since established successfully their right to sue their own governments under Community law through domestic courts; and domestic courts have both accepted the supremacy of Community law and referred upward to the ECJ in cases in which the correct ruling is unclear. The ECJ's power of interpretation has thus become a significant factor in the evolution of the Community system, most markedly in developing the principle of mutual recognition (whereby a product lawfully produced and mar-

12. Weiler (1982, 1991); Burley and Mattli (1993). The quotation is from article 31 of the ECSC treaty.

13. *Costa* v. *ENEL*, Case 6/64, ECR 585, 1964.

keted in one state must except under exceptional circumstances be accepted in another member state). The growing volume of cases referred to the Court led to the creation, under the Single European Act, of an ancillary Court of First Instance, empowered to handle, subject to appeal to the ECJ, some aspects of competition law, cases involving Commission staff, and certain issues under the ECSC treaty.

This is a constitutional system, recognizable as such to those with experience of other systems of multilevel government within a federal framework. The resistance of English common lawyers to Community membership, in the early 1960s, on the grounds that the principle of parliamentary sovereignty was incompatible with the acceptance of the superiority of treaty-based law over parliamentary statute, has given way to an acceptance that parliamentary statute can indeed be thus limited. "It is now right to think of the Treaties as part of the [British] Constitution," the British foreign secretary has remarked, implying that Britain has acquired from abroad the first elements of a written constitution, complete with an external sovereign.[14] The German Constitutional Court had on successive occasions carefully avoided ruling on the compatibility of Community law with the fundamental rights and freedoms entrenched in the Federal German constitution, until it was presented with a legal challenge to the Maastricht Treaty on European Union. Its ruling on that case (October 12, 1993), setting out a number of conditions on accountability and representation in any further revision of the treaties, has introduced a degree of uncertainty into the process of Community institution-building. It requires the intergovernmental conference planned for 1996 to address itself more directly to the constitutional aspects of treaty revision and to the underlying political character of the Community itself.

The second federal element in the Community model is provided by the European Parliament. Its members were indirectly elected until 1979; its fourth direct election took place in June 1994. The legitimacy of the Parliament is limited by the diverse electoral systems through which it is elected in the different member states, and by a clearly lower turnout for European than for national parliamentary

14. Speech by Secretary of State for Foreign and Commonwealth Affairs, Douglas Hurd, to the Cambridge University Conservative Association, February 7, 1992 by (FCO Verbatim Service).

elections.[15] The Parliament's original powers were almost entirely consultative. But the increasing significance of the Community budget, and of the Parliament's role in agreeing to that budget, have allowed it to accumulate influence—as has its strengthened authority under the Single European Act to approve and amend Community legislation as it passes through the Council. These powers are reinforced under the Treaty on European Union.

The third federal element is provided by the Community budget and by the mechanisms that have grown up to manage and control that budget. Common funding was introduced under the ECSC treaty and reinforced under the Treaties of Rome. A common market unavoidably raises issues of the allocation of tariff revenues; these, together with variable levies on agricultural imports introduced under the Common Agricultural Policy (CAP), formed the basis for the Community's "own resources." French determination to entrench the automatic character of Community funding for the CAP before negotiations for British entry reopened in 1970 led to an extension of the concept of "own resources" to an agreed-upon (and adjustable) proportion of the standardized Community-wide value-added tax. Rising demands for financial transfers within the enlarged Community led in turn to the addition of a "fourth resource" in 1988, a rate levied on national governments on the basis of their share of Community gross domestic production (GDP) at market prices.

As it stood in the early 1990s, the Community budget represented a rudimentary system of fiscal federalism, with many perverse and underdeveloped elements. Well over half of the expenditure still went to support agriculture—a bias that left Denmark and the Netherlands, the richest states within the Community in terms of GDP per head, as net beneficiaries. The growth of financial transfers, together with the impact of agricultural expenditure and the increasingly progressive revenue base, meant, however, that Ireland and Greece were receiving net transfers equivalent to almost 5 percent of their GDP. The Community budget now amounted to over 1 percent of EC GDP—a significant sum, although still far too small to play any major role in macroeconomic management. A Court of Auditors had been

15. The level of turnout for European elections, at 63 percent in 1989 and 57 percent in 1994, is of the same order as that for U.S. presidential elections (with a postwar high of 62.6 percent in 1960) and above that for off-year congressional elections.

created to check on financial disbursements, reporting to the European Parliament and the Council of Ministers.

This extensive and intricate structure of rules and institutions—a proto-government, with varied degrees of authority or impotence over its member nation-states—is a very long way from anything envisaged in the early 1990s in North American or Asia-Pacific formal integration. It is hard to imagine the U.S. Supreme Court accepting the superiority of treaty-made law with the same dexterity as that shown by the German Constitutional Court, or the U.S. Congress admitting the limitations on its autonomy that the British House of Commons has—if on occasions grudgingly—acknowledged. It is indeed hard to imagine the political circumstances under which the states of Western Europe would now manage to agree on the establishment of such structures if they had not grown up with them as they have developed over the past forty years. Along with the advantages of geographical concentration, Western Europe as it faces the problems of managing intensive informal economic integration has inherited the advantages of an institutional framework designed for different and more limited purposes, which can be adapted to present needs.

Cooperative Federalism:
The Interpenetration of National Governments

The development of the Community system has depended crucially upon the involvement of actors from national political systems. National ministers are the most politically important of those drawn in, national officials the most numerous. Around the formal structure of Council meetings and subordinate committees revolve a rising number of interest group representatives and "policy influentials," national politicians, businessmen and their public affairs directors, and trade union leaders. Community policymaking operates through continuous consultation and bargaining among a large number of nationally based public and private actors, who interact around the table in formal meetings in Brussels, in less formal group meetings outside Brussels, in bilateral contacts in each others' capitals, over the telephone and by fax and telex— often, for those heavily involved in preparing or managing Community policies, several times a day.

The growth of the specifically Community-level institutions—Commission, Court, Parliament—has been paralleled by the growth of this vast network of transnational and transgovernmental interactions, dwarfing the modest staff of the Community institutions in terms of the numbers involved and fundamentally transforming the operations of national government in the EC member states.[16] The EC as a system of managing intensive interdependence, or "deep" integration, is *not*, as the APEC Eminent Persons Group suggests, characterized by "an embracing bureaucracy" centered on the Commission.[17] It operates through active engagement among national administrations, orchestrated by the Commission and the Council Secretariat. As noted earlier in this chapter, it would be difficult for either NAFTA or APEC to move far down the path toward managed regional integration without developing the same network.

The transformation of the EC from the small body with limited legal competences of the early 1960s to the extensive and unwieldy bureaucratic-political system of the 1990s—its buildings spreading across an entire quarter of Brussels—has depended upon the communication revolution which has made it possible for officials and interest group representatives in different states to keep in constant contact with each other, exchanging information and ideas, drawing up joint proposals, building informal coalitions, consulting on agendas and on the interpretation of decisions already made. Senior officials and ministers, as well as their counterparts in the higher levels of the private sector, take it for granted that they travel to Brussels or to other EC capitals in the course of their regular duties one or two days a week. Staff from their permanent missions in Brussels travel back to their own national capitals each week, to sit in on the meetings that draft their own negotiating instructions.

West European integration began as an economic enterprise under American political sponsorship, but its underlying purposes were always as much political as economic. The pursuit of shared political objectives combined with the need to manage the political implications of economic and technical change to foster the development of parallel consultative mechanisms outside the framework of the treaties, which have now become significant dimensions of Western

16. I am relying in these paragraphs in particular on work by Wolfgang Wessels; see Wessels (1991a, b). See also William Wallace (1984, 1986, 1992).

17. Asia-Pacific Economic Cooperation (1993, p.57).

Europe's developing institutional structure. The West European model is not therefore one only of deep economic integration. The interpenetration of governments has gradually extended well beyond the sphere of economic policy to touch on other core areas of national administration.

European political cooperation(EPC) among foreign ministries, deliberately promoted by President de Gaulle and his successors as an intergovernmental enterprise, began in 1970 as a conference of foreign ministers that was to meet at least twice a year. Other participating governments were suspicious at first that this development risked challenging the United States' established position in foreign and defense policy, exercised through the North Atlantic Treaty Organization (NATO). However, German pursuit of a West European *Ostpolitik*, integrating political, security, and economic relations through what became the Conference on Security and Cooperation in Europe gave this new mechanism a purpose, and a direct link to the economic competences of the EC. EPC in the 1970s thus rapidly developed a substructure of committees and working groups, serviced in rotation by officials from the foreign ministry holding the six-monthly EC Council and EPC presidency. A secure telex network followed, linking the participating foreign ministries for the circulation of drafts and reports through bilateral embassies, managed on behalf of the group by the Dutch foreign ministry. A small and mobile group of seconded diplomats was then added to assist the foreign ministry in the chair with preparing and servicing its expanding business; the group institutionalized as a secretariat in Brussels under the Single European Act. This growing secretariat was then integrated into the Council Secretariat under the Maastricht Treaty. [18]

Cooperation in defense and defense procurement began with ad hoc committees and loose organizations within the overall framework of NATO: the Western European Union (WEU), the Eurogroup (from 1969), and the Independent European Programme Group (from 1976). The "revival" of the WEU in 1984 increased the pace both of ministerial meetings and of meetings of subordinate working groups, their complexity increased by the long-standing disagreement between Britain and France on association with NATO. Britain preferred meetings clearly within the NATO institutional framework;

18. De Schoutheete (1986).

France insisted on separate "European" bodies. These too were gathered into the overall framework of the Maastricht Treaty, which agreed among other matters to move the WEU secretariat from London to Brussels—though not yet to merge it into the Council Secretariat.[19]

Intergovernmental cooperation among national ministries of interior and justice, with their associated intelligence and police agencies, had begun in the early 1970s in response to increasing cross-border terrorism and drug trafficking—partly among EC members within the framework of EPC, partly within the wider framework of the Council of Europe. More discreet in their operation even than consultations among foreign ministries, these meetings gradually grew in intensity and range as the problems they faced became more demanding and as the habit of working together became a familiar part of national administration. These too were gathered into the framework of the Treaty on European Union, under Title VI, "Provisions on cooperation in the fields of justice and home affairs."[20]

Observers from outside Europe should note the trends both to broaden the scope of cooperation among this defined group of states and to bring these other dimensions of intergovernmental cooperation within the broader framework of the European Union. The complexities of bargaining across so many sectors among a widening group of governments have led to repeated proposals for "variable geometry" in institutional arrangements and participation, with different groupings and different obligations for different sectors.[21] But the linkages between different issue areas, and the advantages that broad mutual obligations bring to the process of continuous negotiation that constitutes European policymaking, have operated to limit tendencies toward institutional diversity. Smaller groups have from time to time moved ahead of the rest, as on monetary cooperation and removal of internal border controls, but the incentives for other states to join them rather than to accept exclusion have proved strong.

The volume that these interactions among officials and private actors have now reached, and their implications for traditional understanding of autonomous national government, have scarcely been grasped by national parliaments within the EC, let alone by observers

19. Forster, Menon, and Wallace (1992).
20. Anderson and den Boer (1994).
21. Helen Wallace and Ridley (1985).

in third countries. Much of the business transacted is confidential. European Councils drawing together heads of government and major Council of Ministers meetings attract the attention of the media; but the frequent meetings of such arcane bodies as the EC management committee for cereals, the EPC working group on the Middle East, the Article 113 Committee (on international economic relations—a highly important forum for bargaining on such matters as the General Agreement on Tariffs and Trade and U.S.-EC issues), the Economic Policy Committee, and even the Council of Ministers (Transport) or (Research and Development) take place largely unreported and unrecognized.

A survey by Wolfgang Wessels of the full range of meetings that took place in 1985, before the surge of increased activity that followed the Single European Act and the launch of the 1992 Program, noted seventy Councils of Ministers (in around 220 working days) over a twelve-month period, meeting in sixteen different functional Councils, some meeting once or twice a year and others (like the Foreign Affairs/General Council, Agriculture, and Finance) much more regularly.[22] With parallel ministerial meetings within the EPC framework, WEU, Council of Europe, and Organization for Economic Cooperation and Development (OECD), a substantial majority of cabinet ministers of West European national governments were thus engaged in regular multilateral consultations and negotiations. The workload was heaviest for foreign ministers, but such meetings were also a major preoccupation for ministers of finance, trade and industry, and agriculture (of course), and increasingly for ministers of defense, interior and justice, environment, and transport.

Underneath this ministerial multilateral network Wessels listed 537 Commission "expert groups" formulating proposals for the Council, holding 3,364 sessions; 180 committees and working groups under the Council of Ministers, holding 2,072 meetings over the year; 244 implementation committees; and 385 committees and working groups within the NATO framework, 200 within OECD, and 152 within the Council of Europe. He estimates that some 60 percent of the 4,000 senior civil servants in Bonn were directly involved in these meetings, spread across every federal ministry. This level of activity indicates a network of over 25,000 national officials within the EC, with perhaps

22. Wessels (1991a).

another 2,000 to 3,000 from the less actively involved EFTA countries. Not entirely surprisingly, he detected a plateau effect in the growth in frequency of meetings. Beyond a certain point it becomes difficult for an official to operate effectively at two levels; British officials have remarked that it is possible to attend properly to one's national functions with up to two days a week of multilateral business and travel; beyond that point one's ability to manage affairs at the national level unavoidably suffers.[23]

What has developed is in effect a process of continuous multilateral bargaining, in which exchange of information, building up of credit in some areas for use in others, temporary and permanent coalition-building, and extensive collaboration interspersed with occasional confrontation characterize the policy style. Players need to develop a range of negotiating skills; group dynamics and personal relations matter, reputations can be built or undermined, trade-offs searched for, coalition bargains struck.[24] Participating governments need highly competent and multiskilled administrations—and ministers. Knowledge of two or three foreign languages is an asset; monolingual participants lose out on side conversations and casual comments. Familiarity with the domestic constraints under which others operate, the particularities of their administrative structure and style, and the strengths and weaknesses of their government coalitions are advantages. The training of administrators in West European states, and increasingly also of customs officials and military and police officers has therefore altered significantly over the past twenty years. Ministers are in principle supposed to bring their political skills with them into office, though discreet language training is sometimes provided to those moving into posts with particularly heavy multilateral diaries.[25]

23. Personal interviews. See also Wessels (1991a, pp. 232–35). Jeff Stacey, currently a graduate student at Oxford University, has attempted to update these figures for 1991–92 from internal Commission records. He found that the number of Council meetings, under different headings, had risen to 130 a year but that the number of Commission working group sessions had declined, to 2,292 for 1991 and 1,128 for the first six months of 1992—a finding that supports the impression that a plateau of manageable activity had been reached.

24. Helen Wallace (1989, 1991a); de Schoutheete (1991).

25. Development of "informal Councils," for which ministers gather in a comfortable hotel or chateau over a weekend to discuss longer-term issues without a formal agenda and without a tail of supporting officials, has increased the premium on linguistic ability; the model for these was the Gymnich meeting, an innovation of Hans-Dietrich Genscher in the EPC context in 1974. English is the most widely used *lingua franca*, but French and German are also much in evidence, and fluency in other languages can gain their users friends; those who have to wait for the interpreters lose reaction time in informal discussions.

In such a collaborative system, compliance depends upon mutual trust in the integrity of national administrative and legal services, supported by sufficient transparency in national administrative actions and by the right of other governments, companies, or individuals to make legal challenges. The opacity of the relationship between the Italian state and its state-owned banks and industries was a repeated source of grievance to its partners in the 1970s and 1980s. One British diplomat described his functions in the Rome embassy as "industrial espionage," attempting to discover the prices at which, for example, steel was transferred to white goods and car manufacturers in order to build a case on state subsidies and distortion of competition.[26]

Neither the Greek nor the Portuguese administrations were equipped to cope with the complexities of EC policymaking and implementation when they entered the Community in 1981 and 1986, respectively. The Spanish, with greater human and financial resources, had conducted a large-scale preparatory training program. To the irritation of other member states and of the Community institutions, Greek administrative (and political) practices still remained ill adapted for Community collaboration after more than a decade of membership. Doubts about the pace at which the former socialist states of east-central Europe might successfully adapt to shouldering the full obligations of Community membership partly focus on the scale— and depth—of the administrative adaptation required.[27]

One of the most remarkable aspects of formal European integration, nevertheless, is the generally high level of compliance and implementation of Community rules throughout the EC—and increasingly in the neighboring countries around the EC. The rule of Community law throughout Western Europe compares moderately well to the level of implementation of federal law in the southern United States half a century ago. Directly applicable Community *regulations* are enforced through national courts under the oversight of the European Court of Justice. Community *directives,* in which the mechanisms for implementing decisions made at the EC level are left to national governments, present a more mixed record. Monitoring

26. Personal information (1983). See also William Wallace (1984).

27. The Polish secretary of state for European integration estimated at a Salzburg Seminar in July 1993 that his government would need to train four hundred young people a year for ten years in order to create the cadre required to staff Polish ministries and agencies dealing with the EC and to provide Polish recruits for Community institutions.

by the Commission (in its role as "guardian of the treaties") and by the European Parliament of patterns of national implementation of directives was stepped up as the 1992 Program moved forward. The Commission's authority to take member governments to the ECJ for "infringement of Community law" was strengthened further under the Maastricht Treaty (a revision of article 171 of the EC Treaty) by granting it the power to propose financial penalties against defaulting states. The Commission's own assessment at the end of 1993 was that "the situation regarding the observance of Community law and the implementation of directives is relatively satisfactory," although there remained "persistent problems in certain fields" and with certain governments.[28]

Such a high degree of interpenetration of national governments carries with it a substantial disaggregation of the nation-state. West European states cannot be seen in their relations with each other as coherent and coordinated entities negotiating over well-defined *national* interests. Transgovernmental coalitions take shape at senior and junior levels; institutional coalitions form around shared sectional interests. The strength of the agricultural coalition is apparent: deeply entrenched across the Community, rooted in national ministries and in DG-6 of the Commission (the Directorate-General for Agriculture), but drawing also on a tight network of national agricultural organizations and on their European federations and branching out into the agricultural committees of national parliaments and of the European Parliament. Other functional coalitions, of expertise and interest, are apparent in defense and policing, in monetary policy and currency management—despite some sharp differences of interest on occasion. In bilateral summits between France and Germany, and less frequently between Britain and Germany and Britain and France, groups of Cabinet ministers meet together around the table, with defense ministers supporting each other against finance ministers and finance ministers supporting each other against ministers of agriculture.

Officials and ministers need to get to know each other to operate effectively within such a confederal system. But "group-think" then develops; officials who exchange ideas and information feed up to their ministers negotiating briefs that already reflect the developing

28. Commission of the European Communities (1994), p. 6.

consensus and exclude alternative approaches. Joint training schemes were developed in the 1970s to build the basis for easier multilateral collaboration, and exchanges of officials began to follow during the 1980s. Governments thus gained the advantages of having within their ranks people who understood in great detail the assumptions and working practices of other administrations—at the cost that other administrations also understood a great deal about theirs.[29]

The functional approach to international integration was intended by its proponents to replace the solidarity of national interest with the promotion of common functional interests on a wider stage. The European Commission set out to encourage close relationships with Community-level interest organizations, offering them privileged access to the consultative and policymaking processes. But what has followed has not been entirely in accordance with functionalist theory. Brussels is filled with the representatives of interest group confederations, the public affairs representatives of multinational companies, and the lawyers, consultants, and lobbyists who advise them.

These group representatives have not, however, simply transferred their loyalties from the national to the Community level. They have learned how to play on both levels and across the levels, lobbying their national governments (and on occasion other governments as well) against common proposals that do not fit their particular interests, while lobbying in Brussels against obstructive national governments and for Community proposals that protect their interests. The result has been a highly disaggregated policy process, in which the organized interests that have gathered around established common policies operate to resist redistribution of costs and benefits and also to resist the overriding of sectional policies in the furtherance of wider aims.

29. One senior official in the British treasury remarked to the author in the late 1980s on the advantages of having within his division a young man who had taken the course for civil servants from other EC countries at the École Nationale d'Administration and had become good friends with several of his German opposite numbers: "He is very good at telling me in advance what's going to be the German position. My only worry is, what's he telling them in return?" In the winter of 1993 a German diplomat was working in the British Foreign Office Planning Staff; he was the fourth German diplomat to work on exchange for a year inside the Foreign Office in London. Other exchanges were under way among central ministries in Paris, Bonn, London, and other capitals, accompanied by growing cooperation among embassies in third countries, extending in some instances to shared buildings and support services.

Confederations are ill equipped to address redistributive issues and major shifts of direction. They are particularly poor at managing shifts in external relations, since the complexity of the bargaining among those around the table leaves little room to make concessions to those who are outside the room. But those who are familiar with the disaggregated policy processes of Washington—the entrenched coalitions of interests that stretch into government agencies and congressional committees, the immense political effort it requires even for a directly elected president with a substantial staff to overturn established policy and launch a major new initiative, whether domestic or international—will hesitate to criticize the Brussels policy process too sharply. Federal governments have structural weaknesses. Confederal governments exhibit the same weaknesses in magnified form.

The Wider Western Europe: The European Community and Its Neighbors

The EC has never included the whole of the West European region within its boundaries. It began as an inner group of six within the wider sixteen-member Organization for European Economic Cooperation (OEEC). Out of the failure of negotiations for a wider (Western) European Free Trade Area in 1956–57 emerged a residual seven-country EFTA alongside the six-country EEC. The relationship between the EC and the rest of OEEC Europe from then on has been not unlike that between the United States and Canada: one between a dominant core economy and a rich but dependent periphery, attempting to preserve distinctive aspects of preferred social and industrial policies, as well as distinctive foreign policies and external links, while in other respects benefiting as closely as possible from economic and social interaction with the larger neighbor.

The distinction between the EC and EFTA lay in the political objectives and obligations of the former and the determinedly limited economic objectives of the latter. The EFTA states established only a small secretariat (in Geneva) to service their convention. There was to be no invasion of national sovereignty or transfer of negotiating authority. The secretariat was concerned simply with the management of meetings and the provision of papers—though this latter responsibility developed into a research and information function for these small governments in managing their relations with each other and with the EC.

There was never the faintest suggestion at the outset that this geographically dispersed group of countries would need their own court or system of law. Yet there was an underlying consensus on political and economic values, expressed through membership in the parallel Council of Europe, which brought together ministers, parliamentarians, and officials from EC and EFTA member states to discuss such sensitive political issues as civil rights and national education, and that served as a framework for intergovernmental consultations on a wide range of issues, from European surface transport to cross-border crime, migration, and refugees. The European Commission on Human Rights and the European Court on Human Rights were established under this body, limiting the sovereignty of member states in central issues of domestic jurisdiction.[30] The rich Alpine and Nordic democracies were active in pursuing the failings of their poorer Mediterranean counterparts through the rules and supervisory activities that the Council of Europe had established, although Portugal, a founding member (under British sponsorship) of EFTA, benefited from a good deal of tactful tolerance until the collapse of its authoritarian regime in 1975.

Bilateral industrial free trade agreements between the EFTA states and the EC—signed in 1972 by those EFTA members that were not attempting to follow Britain and Denmark (and Norway, whose voters rejected the terms of entry in a referendum)—were sufficient for the economic and industrial circumstances of the 1970s. They allowed EFTA states to continue to pursue their own varieties of social and industrial corporatism, provide high levels of support to their Alpine and Arctic agricultures, maintain (with the exception of Norway and Iceland) their commitment to neutrality, and nevertheless gain from free access to Community markets—which had already

30. Over the past forty years the British government has been repeatedly embarrassed by rulings from the European Court on Human Rights. The absence of any constitutional document in English domestic law that could serve as the basis for legal challenges to state actions on grounds of abuse of fundamental rights has led litigants from that country to appeal more frequently to this other European Court than those from any other country. By the 1980s a rising number of English lawyers and constitutional reformers were therefore calling for the European Convention on Human Rights to be incorporated directly into British law—a step that would provide a second instance of Britain in effect importing elements of a written constitution through the operations of formal integrative structures.

taken over half of their exports in the 1950s and whose share of EFTA exports (for all except Finland) had risen by the 1970s to 60 percent or more.[31] The EFTA states were, in effect, free riders on the West European economic system, and—apart from Norway and Portugal—free riders also on the Western alliance system. They were able to benefit from the evolution of deeper integration within the EC without having to accept the countervailing obligations that full membership entailed.

But development of new fields of Community activity in the late 1970s and early 1980s, together with changes in the technological, managerial, and financial context within which private and state-owned companies from the EFTA states were operating, left their governments less and less satisfied with their peripheral position. Major companies based within these small states became more and more preoccupied with Europe-wide issues. Per Gyllenhammer, chairman of (Swedish) Volvo, was a key figure in the Round Table of European Industrialists formed at the beginning of the 1980s to raise governments' awareness of the need for more positive industrial policies and for greater cross-border infrastructure investment within the EC.[32]

Access to Community research and development programs could be negotiated case by case; but the evolution of Community regulation, law, and practice was forcing EFTA states unilaterally to incorporate Community rules into their domestic legislation without gaining security of market access in return. The "judicial disequilibrium" that resulted from the application of Community law to EC-EFTA trade, and the entrenched advantages that EC governments and companies had in appealing to the ECJ for adjudication in disputed cases, left EFTA countries "in an intolerable situation."[33] EFTA states found themselves caught within a regime designed only for managing shallow integration while unable to avoid the issues of deeper integration with which the EC was grappling: no longer free riders, but disadvantaged rule-takers alongside a more powerful multilateral institution.

Recognition on both sides of the inadequacy of existing arrangements culminated in a ground-breaking EC-EFTA ministerial meeting in April 1984, which issued the Luxembourg Declaration

31. Wijkman (1991).
32. Sharp and Shearman (1987, pp. 49–50); Green (1993).
33. Weiss (1991, p. 250).

committing the participating governments to establish a European Economic Space including the territory of all eighteen states. The declaration underlined the EFTA states' concern to benefit from the full implications of the Community's "four freedoms" (of goods, services, capital, and labor) as well as from the "flanking policies" the Community was developing in support of economic integration—in research and development, information, education and training, environmental protection, support for small companies, consumer protection, promotion of tourism, audiovisual policies, and cooperation over civil protection and emergencies. As the EC moved toward liberalizing access to public procurement contracts there were additional requests from EFTA governments and companies—ABB/Brown Boveri, Eriksson, Nokia, and other companies with major interests in telecommunications and power supply—for further integrative measures. The launching of the 1992 Program exerted further pressure; so did the ECJ's effective assertion of extraterritorial jurisdiction in the "wood pulp" case of 1988, in which it imposed fines on a number of North American and Nordic producers for collaborative actions that had affected prices within the Community.

An accumulation of piecemeal EC-EFTA agreements—on such issues as the simplification of customs and tax documents, transit, mutual recognition of tests on pharmaceutical and food products, and rules of origin—culminated in a proposal from the president of the EC Commission, Jacques Delors, for the negotiation of "a more structured partnership with common decisionmaking and administrative institutions." He saw it as desirable from the Community's perspective to pull together the increasingly complex relationships between different areas of Community policy and EFTA associates. Many observers also saw the Delors proposals as "a pre-emptive strike" to divert the EFTA governments from moving toward full membership applications at a time when the Community was fully occupied with internal consolidation, by holding out the prospect of a viable alternative to membership.[34] Negotiations followed on an ambitious European economic area agreement, through which EFTA governments hoped to gain many of the benefits of membership, and to accept many of its responsibilities, without committing themselves

---

34. Michalski and Wallace (1992, p. 132).

to the political obligations and the formal limitations of sovereignty that full membership would imply.[35]

It proved impossible to square the circle. Economic integration without political integration was the aim, but participation in the formulation and adjudication of Community policies without commitment to the Community's underlying obligations was not attainable. Agreement was reached on a long list of policy areas, from border formalities and customs cooperation through limitations on state aid to industry and state commercial monopolies to freedom of professional establishment and liberalization of financial services (an issue of particular sensitivity for Switzerland). EFTA governments agreed to contribute to financial transfers to the less-developed southern states of the EC—a major concession, accepting as it did the promise that the benefits that EFTA states derived from access to the single market carried with them a share of the EC's financial responsibilities. Fisheries questions proved particularly difficult, given their importance to economic and social priorities in Norway and Iceland; the Community refused to allow full access to EC markets without greater EC access to Norwegian and Icelandic waters. But the insuperable stumbling block was institutional and legal.

EFTA states were asking, in effect, for joint decisionmaking on those issues on which they were willing to accept EC legislation—a very wide agenda—to ensure that the future evolution of Community regulation took their interests into account. To complement that innovation, they wanted direct access to Community lawmaking through the creation of an EEA Court alongside, and in conjunction with, the ECJ. The ECJ, which had not been consulted on these intricate negotiations, ruled after their completion in December 1991 that the formula for a new EEA court was incompatible with the Community treaties, insofar as interpretation of EEA legislation might conflict with interpretation of EC legislation, given the different objectives of the EC and the EEA. The EFTA governments were in effect asking for EEA law to merge with EC law within a common jurisdiction, in spite of the weaker political foundations of the EEA— a proposition that would have proved immensely complex to realize if the ECJ had not struck it down.

35. Helen Wallace (1991b, pp. 240–43).

The EEA Agreement of 1992 therefore emerged with a looser institutional structure, less satisfactory for the EFTA states but achieved without altering the legal and political structure of the Community. There was to be an EEA Council, supported by an EEA Joint Committee, shadowing the EC Council of Ministers and Committee of Permanent Representatives, with the prospect of a succession of subordinate working groups paralleling those that already existed within the Community. The EFTA states agreed to strengthen their own weak central institutions substantially, setting up a new EFTA Surveillance Authority in pale imitation of the Commission, a collegiate body whose members were to be responsible for ensuring that obligations were fulfilled and rules implemented. There was also to be an EFTA Court that would, together with the EC Court of Justice, ensure judicial control of the proper functioning of the EEA Agreement.[36] In addition there would be an EEA Joint Parliamentary Committee, although the intergovernmental character of EFTA meant that no EFTA Parliamentary Assembly was to be formed and the right to approve new legislation was retained by national parliaments.

What had begun as an attempt to define an alternative to full Community membership thus ended in an unsatisfactory compromise, which persuaded almost all the EFTA member governments and all of their business organizations that there *was* in effect no viable alternative to full membership—no halfway house between dependent association and acceptance of the political as well as economic obligations of formal integration. As the negotiations proceeded Sweden, Finland, and Norway therefore followed Austria in applying for full EC membership, their shift of approach greatly eased by the disappearance of the political inhibitions represented by their neutral stance within the East-West conflict. The Swiss government was only prevented from following suit, at the end of 1992, by the rejection of the EEA Agreement by the majority of cantons in a referendum.

There are lessons here for the evolution of institutional and legal integration in other international regions, perhaps most directly in North America. Deep integration, it is clear, involves hard trade-offs between sovereignty and participation in joint policymaking, between the preservation of valued areas of national autonomy and demands for access to other countries' national markets. It is not easy for small

36. EEA Agreement (1993). Other information in this paragraph is taken from other publications of the EFTA Secretariat (1993); see also O'Keeffe (1993).

countries to strike a trade-off acceptable at once to their populations, their economic elites, and the governments and interests of their dominant neighbors. The Swiss and Austrian governments, accustomed from their own federal systems to common jurisdiction among multilevel governments, had pressed for a single common jurisdiction encompassing the EC and EFTA, recognizing that an adjudication system between the EC and EFTA would leave the EC as the more powerful party, with a strong possibility that its preferences would therefore prevail in cases of dispute.

Tighter formal legal integration was therefore in the interests of these smaller states: institutions matter, in particular in protecting smaller states from their larger neighbors. But larger confederations— or federations—see little advantage in giving others a share in jurisdiction over their internal affairs without the others accepting political obligations in return. It is evidently to the advantage of Canada and Mexico for NAFTA rules to be adjudicated through a formal legal process rather than through the semipolitical processes of intergovernmental arbitration. It is easy, however, to anticipate the reaction of the U.S. Supreme Court to any proposal to establish such a NAFTA Court with parallel jurisdiction.[37]

In the winter of 1993–94 EFTA governments thus negotiated terms for accession to full membership of the EC. Parties and politicians previously opposed to full membership as too costly to national autonomy shifted ground and set out to convince first the EC and then their national electorates that the benefits to be gained from thus compromising sovereignty were now greater than the political and psychological costs. Economic integration, it had become clear to them, was not separable from political integration, nor multilateral economic cooperation from political and security obligations. In briefing EC governments in early 1994 the Swedish government laid particular emphasis on the scale of its contribution to the Nordic battalion in Bosnia, as symbolizing its willingness to accept its share of common European responsibilities. The December 1993 elections in Russia, and the emergence of Vladimir Zhirinovsky, were reflected in a sharp

37. Justice Scalia's remark in *Thompson* v. *Oklahoma*, 487 U.S. 815, 868, note 4 (1988), that "where there is not first a settled consensus among our own people, the views of other nations, however enlightened the Justices of this Court may think them to be, cannot be imposed upon Americans" indicates a deep-seated resistance to acceptance of international law within the jurisdiction of the United States; see also Koh (1991).

shift in opinion polls in Finland and Sweden in favor of Community membership, political and security considerations persuading many unconvinced by economic arguments alone that incorporation into a larger entity was advantageous. Yet the outcome of referenda to ratify Community membership, due in all the EFTA applicants in the autumn of 1994, remained in doubt. The limits of integration among democratic states are set largely by what national publics will accept, and by popular fears about the erosion of political and cultural autonomy.

Chapter 4

The Limits of Integration

*T*HE transformation of the West European economy from the mixture of heavy industry and agriculture of the 1950s to the advanced manufacturing and service economy of the 1990s has carried with it a transformation—and a massive widening—of the agenda of formal integration. The transformation of societies in West European democracies through education, affluence, and mass (national and international) communication has brought a range of further issues into regional international politics. Within this geographically compact group of densely populated states, cross-border economic and social interactions have risen to levels that have pushed governments into setting up new institutions for collective management.

The experience of West European integration in the 1970s and 1980s suggests that the process of deepening integration beyond the initial removal of tariff barriers has no easily definable limits. Each new issue on the intergovernmental agenda penetrates further into sensitive areas of domestic politics, into the distinctive and divergent traditions of state and local administration, of the relationship between state and market and of the relationship between social and economic priorities. It is a process in which economic and administrative logics, political realities, and popular acceptability frequently pull in different directions. Adoption of common policies in one area increases pressure for common policies in related areas—a process that at once demonstrates "spillover" from already common policies and "spillback" from the disruptive effect of unharmonized national policy decisions on areas already harmonized.

Successive attempts since 1970 to move toward monetary union without parallel moves toward a wider economic union provide the classic example of this complex interaction of economic and political imperatives. Economic arguments for currency stability within the region, most efficiently for a single currency, have become more persuasive as the regional economy has become more closely integrated. Bargaining over the terms and conditions of moves toward a single currency has, however, unavoidably spilled over into related areas, with economically stronger governments pressing for European Community (EC) controls on national economic management and fiscal balances, and economically weaker governments demanding compensatory financial transfers in return for accepting the disciplines imposed. Issues of sovereignty, popular identification with familiar national currencies, and the distinctive views of national political cultures on the social impact of such developments or the permissibility of moderate inflation further complicate and confuse attempts to contain the issues under negotiation.

Politics—domestic politics within member states and increasingly also political activities that cross borders among different member states—sets the agenda for regional intergovernmental negotiation as much as administrative or economic logic. The existence and momentum of European institutions have attracted the attention of lobbyists, campaigning groups, and activist national politicians. Successful political institutions tend to expand their authority and their sphere of action; spillover takes place from one issue area to another not just because different areas are linked but also because political actors will seek out rulemakers who seem to them best placed to lay down and implement the rules they wish to impose.

Over the thirty-five years since the Treaties of Rome came into operation the number of issues with which the Community is concerned, and the competences that it has acquired to manage them, have grown immensely. Together with the other more intergovernmental West European institutions, the region has developed structures for joint decisionmaking and joint implementation that reach down into the depths of national sovereignty and domestic politics. But the integration of governments, supported by the growth of Europe-wide lobbies, has not provided the basis for an effective or popularly accepted new political system. The remoteness of the policymaking process from national politics, the obscurities both of the complex committee structure and of so many of the issues under negotiation, breed popular suspicion. The sense that increasingly central, or symbolic, aspects of national life are being controlled and changed by shadowy groups of civil servants and secret deals between "our" ministers and foreign politicians has raised fears about national autonomy and national identity.

The institutional framework for West European integration represented a carefully constructed compromise between sovereignty and federation, in which the governments of participating states negotiated to gain as many of the benefits of integration as possible while yielding as little as they might of national autonomy.[1] Commitment to "ever-closer union" was deliberately ambiguous, broad enough to satisfy the idealists who looked ahead to a United States of Europe, the technocrats who believed that enlightened and efficient administration would displace partisan national politics, and the national politicians seeking to strike a limited bargain for mutual advantage. European integration has moved forward through a succession of further formal limited bargains. These carefully assembled package deals among governments began in the 1980s to be incorporated into revisions of the original treaties, to ensure effective implementation. The Maastricht Treaty on European Union was thus only a further stage in a succession of hard-negotiated bargains that had begun with the treaties themselves and had moved through the "Hague package" of December 1969 through the more limited agreements of 1970s European Councils to the 1987 Single European Act and the Maastricht Treaty.

Multi-issue bargaining among governments pursuing ambiguous and partly contradictory objectives, conducted largely behind closed doors, does not, however, reassure national electorates. They perceive that more and more of the regulations and policies that affect their daily lives are being removed from the purview of local and national government to Brussels. But they have little sense of understanding— let alone participating in—this remote, Brussels-centered policy process; only aware that their national governments are less and less able to deliver the programs for national economic and social improvement on which they win and lose elections. Trust between national elites and national electorates has thus been weakened across Western

1. This argument is made most powerfully in Milward (1992); Milward and others (1993).

Europe, without a compensating strengthening of trust in this new level of government that has emerged above the national level. The revival of regional and separatist movements within several West European states partly reflects the recognition that the nation-state is no longer so central to national security and prosperity; it also reflects the limited appeal of "Europe" as an idea and of the EC as an alternative focus for loyalty.

Divergent political, economic, and social pressures thus mark the shifting limits of West European integration. The politics of West European integration are, to a substantial extent, about where those limits should be set; the national politics of West European states are also increasingly focused around this question. Intensive patterns of interdependence that grew up within the institutional framework established under the original treaties, intensified further by techno-logical and industrial changes in the 1970s and 1980s and above all by the revolution in communications, have pushed governments into new fields of cooperation, regulation, and common policies. Bargain-ing over the perceived distribution of costs and benefits from the rules and policies under negotiation has brought questions of financial compensation and transfers into the balance—as in national and federal politics in more strongly established political systems.

The relatively weak institutionalization of this regional political system in comparison to explicit federations has, however, meant that disagreements over institutions themselves and over the assignment of competence over particular policy areas among the different levels of government have also become a central focus for Community politics. Among the wider public, largely excluded from a system of government that has integrated national administrations without inte-grating national politics, there is uncertainty and alienation: a sense of lost autonomy that amounts almost to a crisis of confidence in na-tional government, and even approaches a crisis of national identity within several of the member states.

From Negative to Positive Integration

The rationalistic administrators who set the tone for the European Commission in its early years were endowed with the faith that most major issues would be more effectively managed at the Community level than at the national, and that they could be managed at the Community level in a less partisan fashion than was characteristic of national politics.[2] But the number of issues that needed to be handled at the European level in the early 1960s remained very limited. The national base and predominantly national ownership of industrial companies, banks, and service agencies meant that issues of competition policy and social and employment regulation, though included within the Treaties of Rome (articles 89–94 and 117–22), remained for the most part national in focus. Patterns of communication and travel were mostly contained within national boundaries. What little environmental regulation there was was the responsibility of local government more often than national.

The treaty establishing the European Economic Community (EEC) envisaged the development of common policies in a wide range of fields apart from those that flowed directly from the removal of barriers to internal trade and from allowing the free movement of persons, services, and capital throughout the Community: agriculture, transport, competition, tax harmonization, cooperation in economic policy, and a range of social and employment issues (including "the application of the principle that men and women should receive equal pay for equal work" and financial assistance with structural adjustment and for the retraining of workers from displaced industries. Pressure from the Dutch, in particular, to open German markets to Dutch agricultural exports in return for opening Dutch markets to German industrial goods, had led to the inclusion of agriculture in the treaty; a Franco-Dutch coalition thereafter drove through a detailed set of rules for a common regime for agriculture, transferring this policy sector more effectively than any other (apart from commercial policy) from the national to the European level.[3]

The failure of the Dutch to find allies in their pursuit of common rules for road and rail transport, in the face of entrenched differences in national assumptions about the regulation and financing of transport, blocked comparable progress in that field for twenty-five years; the stalemate was the result not of rational decision or of careful consideration of the most appropriate level at which the transport sector should be managed, but of a structural and geographical block presented by German assumptions about state railways and French

2. Hallstein (1973, p. 60).
3. Milward (1992, chapter 5). The quotation is from article 119 of the treaty.

assumptions about the maintenance of national licensing and border controls. Only pressure from road haulage companies within France, exerted through blockades of the border roads during the peak of the winter holiday season, shifted national policy. The coalition between the Netherlands and Britain that developed in the 1980s on deregulation of European transport reflected not only the declared economic liberal stance of the two governments but also their particular geographical position. They are both situated on the western edge of the European continent, and they share strong interests in freer transit across it, just as those in the center—Germany, Switzerland, and Austria—share interests in controlling and channeling transit across their territories.[4]

The progression from one policy sector to another has followed political priorities and mindsets rather than the principles of rational administration. The most acutely political (and, from some perspectives, irrational) example of spillover was the French drive for monetary union between 1969 and 1972, driven by fears that currency fluctuations would undermine the newly established principles of common agricultural prices and financing.

Removal of tariff and quota barriers to trade, as all states have discovered, only transfers attention to those nontariff barriers that remain, many of which have been erected below the nation-state level by activist local governments. Harmonization of regulations on food hygiene, for instance, in order to permit Community-wide circulation of food products, involved agonizing changes in the profession and hierarchy of local inspection that had grown up across Britain over the previous hundred years. Local restrictions on noise in German towns constituted a barrier to trade against lawnmowers imported from Britain, a country with a higher customary tolerance of interruptions to peaceful weekends, and touched off an intricate negotiation within an expert EC committee on the harmonization of lawnmower noise regulations throughout the EC.

4. The issue of Alpine transit has become one of the most sensitive questions in relations among Austria, Switzerland, and the EC. The environmental implications of unrestricted road transport through the Alpine passes between German and Italy and between Germany and southeastern Europe have aroused passionate local oppositions; making this one of the most difficult dossiers to negotiate in the Austrian application for accession to the EC. The Swiss electorate approved a hugely expensive scheme to build a new rail tunnel under the Alps, to transfer transit traffic from road to rail, in a referendum a few weeks before they narrowly rejected the European Economic Area in 1992.

The deeper the integration of European markets, the more national and local rules that had had their origins in diverse traditions, assumptions, or fears began to be pictured as restraints to trade. The German *Reinheitsgebot,* which banned the sale of any beer that did not satisfy strict standards of purity of ingredients, had its origins in guild regulation and ducal law in sixteenth-century Bavaria; the effective protection it offered against French, Belgian, and British beers reaching German drinkers nevertheless led to its being struck down by the European Court of Justice.[5] Local and national initiatives in the 1980s to raise environmental and recycling standards ran into similar challenges. After tough negotiations at the Luxembourg European Council in December 1985 the Danes were allowed to maintain their ban on the sale of beer in cans, on the grounds that this prohibition applied equally to Danish and non-Danish brewers and contributed to a raising of environmental standards. But enthusiastic German laws on recycling, introduced in 1989–91 without ensuring the provision of sufficient domestic recycling facilities, caused so much disruption in other states—collapse in the price of waste paper, cross-border disposal of waste intended for recycling within Germany—that the issue of national recycling programs was forced onto the EC agenda during 1993.

Negotiations for Swedish entry were overshadowed in the winter of 1993–94 by the question of wet snuff, a national idiosyncracy to which Swedes were strongly attached, but one that fell under a Community ban on chewing tobacco introduced some years earlier on British initiative in response to a rise in mouth cancer in Scotland. The German health minister campaigned within his own government in the spring of 1994 for a ban on the importation of British beef, in response to fears that bovine spongiform encephalopathy, a number of cases of which had been reported in British beef herds, might be transferable to humans. British arguments that no such cases had been discovered were countered by German arguments that no assurance could yet be given that consumption of contaminated meat would *definitely* not transfer the infection. The schism reflects a differ-

5. *Commission* v. *Federal German Republic,* Case 178/84, ECR 1227, 1987. The German government's political position in defending the *Reinheitsgebot* was somewhat weakened by its parallel efforts to defend, against French opposition, the traditional practices of German winemakers in being permitted to "improve" wine by adding sugar and other substances.

ence of philosophical approach to market regulation between the two countries that ranges from health risks to insurance risks.[6]

Rulemaking is a highly political and only partly objective process, in which interested parties play one level against another: using local or national regulations to promote particular interests against the wider Community and Community rules against the particular interests of others. Inclusion of social and employment provisions in the original EEC treaty had reflected nervousness (on the part of the French in particular) about the advantages that would flow to those with less strict employment regulations within a common market unless these were harmonized as integration progressed. Differences in national economic and social structures became more sensitive as economic integration proceeded—and as the Community enlarged to bring in countries with a greater diversity of rules and practices.

There was a substantial degree of similarity among the original Six in terms of relations between state and industry, state and the financial sector, and state and the "social partners," employees and workers' representatives; all were marked to one degree or another by the corporatist tradition and by the influence of Catholic social doctrine. But there were also significant differences, which became both more apparent and more sensitive as economic integration moved on from trade to cross-border manufacturing and service activities. The ethos of German trade unions differed sharply from that of their counterparts in France and Italy for strong historical and political reasons; so did their relationship with employers, with union representatives sitting alongside bankers and businessmen on supervisory boards. The complex relationship between banks and government in Germany sharply differed from the pattern of relations in Italy. The Federal German Economics Ministry's proclaimed commitment to liberal markets was balanced by the substantial federal subsidies provided for steel, railways, Lufthansa, shipbuilding, and other industries, and by extensive public ownership of manufacturing enterprises and banks at the *Land* (state) level. The distinctive relationships between the central bank and the finance ministry in highly centralized France and Federal Germany were marked not only by constitutional structures and divergent assumptions about

6. Albert (1993, chapter 5).

the dangers of inflation but also by different intellectual and public service traditions.[7]

The transformation of the European (and developed global) economy in the 1970s and 1980s under the impact of technical, communications, and managerial changes made such distinctions more sensitive. Pressures for a European company law came partly from rational rulemakers, seeking to encourage cross-border mergers by lowering the barriers presented by different national frameworks. There was also pressure from trade unions representing workers in multinational companies to harmonize rights to representation and to incorporate from more favorable national laws references to the responsibilities of management to employers as well as to shareholders. Divergent national practices on disclosure of financial information and accountancy sank the attempted Dunlop-Pirelli merger in 1981; divergent assumptions about the relationship between financial institutions as shareholders and bankers and the companies in which they invested inflamed the Pirelli bid for Continental in 1990–91. As companies from more "closed" economies bid for takeovers in more open neighbors—Italian companies for German, German and Swiss for British, French state-owned companies for privately owned German and British—those attacked pressed for a leveling of the playing field. The political storm within Britain over the Nestlé takeover of Rowntree in 1988 led to changes in Swiss company law; not that the Swiss government at that point had any intention of joining the Community, but Swiss multinationals were anxious to avoid discriminatory action.

Financial integration followed both from formal rule changes and from the informal impact of electronic transfers and trading. Here again divergent national traditions represented larger and larger obstacles as other barriers came down. The Italian financial structure was clearly incompatible with those of other member states, although it would be difficult to reform without reforming the entire Italian political system. German and British insurance systems started from entirely opposite assumptions about the appropriate distribution of

7. Andrew Shonfield explored these structural differences in a classic study, Shonfield (1965). For a more recent discussion, which distinguishes between different European models as well as between these various European models and American and Japanese politico-economic structures, see Albert (1993). On the social policy sector see Liebfried (1992).

risk and the degree of public oversight needed to protect the public—making it easier for German insurance companies to meet criteria for operation in British markets than vice versa.[8] Swiss insurance companies risked losing their assured access to German markets as a result of harmonization of insurance regulations on a Community basis, a development that touched off a complex and lengthy negotiation that forced the Swiss to make a number of concessions toward the EC consensus.

What is striking about many of these examples is how often West European states have found themselves bargaining to harmonize rules in areas that within the United States remain largely under the jurisdiction of individual states. The absence of a strong central authority, or of large-scale automatic transfers through a federal budget from richer states and regions to poorer ones, make distributive issues more sensitive case by case. Each government has to negotiate to avoid being put at a structural disadvantage, but with insufficient confidence that what it concedes in one negotiation it will regain in others. The disaggregated policy process of Brussels, furthermore, allows interested organizations and the issue coalitions they build to exert powerful influence over specific negotiations, without being counterbalanced by broader political coalitions pursuing wider goals.

Distributive Politics: Core and Periphery

Financial compensation is one instrument for gaining concessions on rules on which the EC has depended from the beginning. The European Coal and Steel Community in effect "bought" Belgian consent to the phasing out of its Walloon coal mines through subsidies for retraining and redeployment. The European Social Fund was included in the EEC treaty as a concession to the Italians, and as an alternative to immediate opening of labor markets in the richer northern countries to emigrants from the Italian south. The Regional Development Fund emerged from the 1971–72 entry negotiations, with British hopes that the flow of funds would counter the perverse impact of the agricultural budget. The Commission, and the Six, attempted to maintain against British complaints in the late 1970s

8. Albert (1993, chapter 5).

that the distribution of agricultural costs and benefits could not be seen in terms of progressive taxation or equitable distribution; but increasingly bitter confrontations about the perverse distribution of budgetary costs and benefits ended in 1984 with effective acceptance of equitable principles. Mediterranean entry further reinforced them, with the Community accepting that financial transfers were a necessary part of the political and economic package that brought these developing countries into the EC and opened their markets to its goods and investment.

Distributional issues and regulatory issues often become entangled. Regulation of "state aid" (subsidies) is caught up with the survival of marginal industries in falling markets and with the competition for multinational investment. The bitter battle over steel subsidies to Ekostahl (the largest steel plant in the former East Germany) in the winter of 1993 involved issues of reconstructing the East German economy and balancing subsidized German plants against privatized British factories, as well as the interests of the Italian company that was then proposing to invest in Ekostahl and the looming problem of accommodating steel imports from Poland within a shrinking EC market. The transfer by the U.S. Hoover company of production facilities from Dijon to Scotland in 1991 brought angry attacks from France against Scottish regional investment incentives and lower social overheads. Divergent Spanish and German positions on the "social charter" were marked by German fears that jobs and investment were flowing out of Germany to countries with lower social and employment standards—to Spain in particular. Spanish determination to entrench the existing pattern of financial flows within the package that concluded the enlargement negotiations with the European Free Trade Association (EFTA) countries, in 1992–93, reflected fears that the shifting balance of a Community that took in first the Nordic and Alpine countries and then the Visegrad countries (Poland, the Czech Republic, Hungary, and Slovakia) would divert investment and trade away from the Iberian Peninsula. Thus insistence on financial compensation was a justified form of self-protection against a shift of balance that it was unable in the long run to prevent.

Limitation of common financing and common expenditures to a small proportion of governmental activity makes it more difficult to agree on appropriate attribution or levels of burden sharing. Military and security expenditures were firmly excluded from the remit of the civilian EC, with defense burden sharing conventionally a matter for transatlantic bargaining between the United States and the three main West European military powers—Britain, Germany, and France, responsible among them for almost two-thirds of West European military spending. Occasional outbursts of irritation within the German government, in the early 1980s, against the Dutch and the Danes—who were both net beneficiaries from the Community budget and made, considering their per capita gross domestic production (GDP), modest contributions to the common defense—did not break out into public confrontation. But in the changed circumstances of the post–cold war era the distribution of military costs and benefits began also to spill over into Community bargaining—despite the careful separation of moves toward a Common Foreign and Security Policy (CFSP) from the EC proper in the three-pillar structure of the Maastricht Treaty. The Belgian government succeeded in negotiating financial support for the dispatch of a battalion to Somalia, in early 1993, from the EC's European Development Fund, on the grounds that it was to be sent in support of developmental objectives.[9] The Spanish government at the same time formally requested a German contribution toward the costs of its troops in Bosnia—although without success. One of the issues that heads of government faced at the Brussels European Council in December 1993 was funding for the expanding CFSP secretariat. Against the resistance of the British government, the institutional walls erected between the different pillars of the European Union (EU) were lowered to allow for the convenience of funding from a common budget, thus providing the European Parliament with a lever that it might use to exert a degree of oversight over its future development.

Financial transfers were thus an essential part of the EC bargain, and they have continued to play an important role in the trade-offs through which common policies are developed. Governments declare their determination to hold the EC budget down, but it continues to drift up, to more than 1 percent of the collective GDP of EC member countries, and the list of areas that the EC is asked to help fund continues to grow. No stable compromise has yet been reached here,

9. In fact it was not dispatched until some months later. Agreement to make a financial contribution was hedged with cautious language on the exceptional circumstances of the present case: clear evidence that those involved were aware that a major precedent was being set.

either. The opening up of the economies of Eastern Europe; their demands for long-term assistance, competing with Mediterranean demands for compensation; and their success in attracting new investment, forcing adjustment in the EC's western regions, will further sharpen the politics of distribution.

The political experience of economic and monetary integration offers another powerful example of the difficulties of finding a stable compromise between sovereignty and federation—and of the destabilizing effects of technological change and of external shocks. It also raises underlying issues about the relationship between the core of the European economy—Germany itself, and the regions and small countries immediately neighboring—and the Mediterranean and western (and future eastern) peripheries. The first attempt to move toward economic and monetary union (EMU) in 1970–73, was sparked partly by the desire to protect European currencies from increasing turbulence in international currency markets and was then sunk by the intensified turbulence that followed the August 1971 decoupling of the dollar from gold—leaving unresolved disputes over what measures of economic policy coordination or fiscal federalism would be needed to accompany monetary union. The European Monetary System (EMS) was launched in March 1979 as a deliberately modest substitute, allowing for adjustments of exchange rates among the participants in response to changes of circumstance or unexpected shocks. The unexpected success of the EMS bred increased confidence in the course of the 1980s, giving rise to a growing reluctance to adjust rates and to implicit assumptions that the Bundesbank would manage the system in the interests of the whole.

Relaunched proposals for EMU in 1988–90 nevertheless reopened underlying issues of power, accountability, objectives, and compensation. The concept of a central bank without a central government, as the former president of the Bundesbank, Karl-Otto Pöhl, was fond of pointing out, was itself open to question: issues of accountability and of maintaining political support for monetary objectives were raised. Relations with subordinate levels of government had to be spelled out—with German insistence on tight borrowing limits for national governments reflecting the country's skepticism that the Italian government was capable except under the most extreme pressure of controlling its budgetary deficit. The breakdown of the Keynesian policy consensus and the shift toward monetarism over the inter-

vening twenty years made questions of compensating fiscal mechanisms less central; but they would undoubtedly have returned to the
center if the external shock of German reunification had not thrown
the EMS out of balance. The initial stance of the German government, that it would yield on the dominance of the deutsche mark and
the Bundesbank in return for real progress toward more democratic
and accountable institutions at the Community level, was a linkage
that was resisted by the French (and British), only to be reiterated in
the final stages of Maastricht Treaty ratification by the German Constitutional Court.

The French attempted to pursue monetary union within strict
limits, not yielding further political sovereignty in return; but that
limitation increased skepticism inside Germany about the costs and
benefits of the trade-off. The widespread German perception that the
deutsche mark is itself a major German asset, even a symbol of
national economic success and financial rectitude, has been compounded by the parallel perception that the German taxpayer is
expected to pay disproportionately to support the economies of the
less efficient and honest member states. German negotiators insisted
in the Maastricht negotiations on strict conditions for inflation rates
and fiscal balances before national currencies were allowed to join the
projected second and third stages of the move toward monetary
union. It seems unavoidable that constitutional, budgetary, monetary,
and economic dossiers will be linked in the scheduled 1996 intergovernmental conference (IGC)—although it is less clear that either
the German government or the German public will still be willing to
trade monetary and economic policy concessions to the French and
others in return for institutional strengthening.

The interests of other smaller and more peripheral states in the side
bargains that would accompany moves toward monetary union are
different from those of France. Awareness of the central position of
the German economy has made them more concerned about the
need to build measures that protect their own economies and political
autonomy from what they see as the threat of German dominance.
The sensitivity of the second home issue (purchases of property as
holiday homes in village and country areas of neighboring states by
nationals of the richer core countries) derives from fear of being
swamped by German money and German values, with German preferences on social legislation and economic policy also being forced

upon them. The rich core countries, in their turn, fear exploitation by their smaller and peripheral partners, successfully extracting side payments in return for each new package of policies that the core countries demand, leaving a budgetary and political balance ever more skewed in their favor. Hence the particular sensitivity of voting rules, as the Community moves toward enlargement to include a succession of smaller countries, both rich and poor. The British government's clumsy attempt to resist any change in the threshold of votes needed for a qualified majority in the final stages of the EFTA enlargement negotiations in March 1994 only irritated both its partners and the applicant states. However, the Ioannina Compromise agreed to at a special Council of Ministers on March 29 made it clear that the whole issue of weighted voting and qualified majorities would be reopened at the 1996 IGC, with the prospect of further enlargement to bring in states from east-central Europe to concentrate attention on the issue.

Multilevel Government: The Joint Decision Trap

Government by intergovernmental committee is unavoidably intricate and opaque. It is hard even for those whose professional responsibility it is to maintain an overview of the business at hand, in prime ministerial offices and permanent representations, to keep abreast of every aspect of Community policymaking, let alone of other intergovernmental negotiations under way in associated areas. The technical nature of most of the dossiers engrosses those involved in them and discourages political oversight. Heads of government may agree to give a new impetus to negotiations in particular areas and under exceptional circumstances (as in the establishment of the EMS in 1979) may override their experts' opinions. But in most instances the dossier, after its brief moment of prime ministerial purview, is recaptured by the experts and the representatives of affected interests, and grinds on toward agreement within the compartmentalized field of intergovernmental business in which it started.[10]

In principle the Commission should provide an overview—a sense of direction, even vision, as those who designed the institutional

10. I am drawing heavily in this section on Scharpf (1988).

structure of the EC envisaged it. But the Commission itself is caught up in detailed dossiers, in the management of the vastly broader agenda with which the EC in the 1990s is now faced, and with the national, intergovernmental, and interest group politics that wider agenda has brought with it. Seventeen Commissioners from twelve states form much less of a "college" than the original nine from six. Individual commissioners are preoccupied with their sectoral responsibilities (as national Cabinet members are with their ministerial responsibilities)—with such complex and time-consuming negotiations as the Uruguay Round of the General Agreement on Tariffs and Trade, the Europe Agreements with the former Eastern Europe, the liberalization of European air transport, the agricultural price round, or the Fourth Framework Program for European research and development.

Commissioners and their cabinets (executive offices) also spend time maintaining links with national governments and politics within their home states—sounding out opinion, "selling" Community policies, nurturing their domestic political base—thus forging a further set of links in the intricate network of multilevel government that the EC constitutes. Directorates-general, in their turn, are functional baronies, locked into close relations with the interests they regulate and the national ministerial departments to which they relate. A strong Commission president, like Jacques Delors, can to some extent reimpose coherence, though in practice Delors has worked most closely with an inner core of commissioners and advisers rather than with the full college, let alone with the twenty-three directorates-general of the Commission as a whole. The Commission president must spend his fund of political credit carefully: assembling coalitions of support for Commission initiatives before they are launched, cultivating national governments while remaining alert to the changing currents of politics within the member states, building up to major initiatives and following each through before any new initiative is contemplated.[11]

Alternative sources of political initiative are to be found in the six-month rotating Council presidency and in sustained coalitions among member governments. The Franco-German coalition, main-

11. I am drawing in this paragraph on the doctoral thesis on presidential leadership in preparation by Ken Endo at Oxford University. Readers will note the (deliberate) echoes of Washington presidential politics here, although the Commission president, appointed rather than elected, has far fewer resources at his disposal in exercising the power to persuade.

tained throughout the 1970s and 1980s through intense bilateral consultation at levels from heads of government on down, has proved effective on many occasions both in pushing proposals forward and in agreeing to hold others back. The three Benelux countries have also sustained the habit of group coordination, although they were far less effective in the Maastricht negotiations than the Franco-German partnership. A British-Italian partnership has surfaced intermittently as an alternative coalition to the Franco-German. A three-government directoire, with Germany, France, and Britain providing concerted leadership, has appeared a possibility on one or two occasions, only to founder on British unfamiliarity with coalition politics.[12]

Council presidencies offer the opportunity for different governments briefly to raise the saliency of their preferred agenda items and to demonstrate to their partners and their domestic publics the quality of their political leadership. Yet all too often the government of the presidency-in-office is caught up in domestic difficulties, forthcoming elections, or even governmental crises, which distract it from Community business. The Greek presidency in the first six months of 1994 was weakened by the ill health of several Greek ministers and the death of one key government member. Hopes that successive German, French, and Spanish presidencies from July 1994 to December 1995 would provide a concerted impetus were diminished by agreement between the French and German governments, incorporated into the "conclusions" of the Ioannina Council of Ministers, that the "reflection group of representatives of foreign ministers" set up by the Corfu European Council (at the conclusion of the Greek presidency) in June 1994 would not start its work until the summer of 1995; that is, it was to be delayed until after both the German Bundestag and French presidential elections.

Commission leadership has been crucial in successive major EC initiatives. For example the Commission and its president played major roles in assembling and promoting the 1992 package, and in launching the EMS proposals in 1978 and the renewed EMU initiative in 1989, although in each of these cases the support of key national governments was essential for success. The Action Plan on Competitiveness, Employment and Growth adopted by the European Council in December 1993 was the culmination of several months of

12. De Schoutheete (1991).

Commission research and consultation with interested organizations and with national ministries, supplemented by preparatory speeches and articles. There is, however, a limit to the number of occasions on which such major initiatives can be mounted and on the number of issues on which they can be focused. As in the more developed federal politics of the United States, the amount of political investment required to promote particular proposals means that other issues have to be left to routine management within the functional coalitions that gather around them.

Problems of direction and leadership are compounded by the lack of clear principles for distributing authority in different policy sectors among the Community, national governments, and subordinate regional and local authorities. Federations assign policy competences among different levels of government through written constitutions, leaving lawyers and politicians to argue over the generations about constitutional interpretation and the requirements of changing circumstances. Foreign policy, money, foreign trade, defense, and the maintenance of order have been the core functions of federations, with commerce and economic regulation left as far as possible to the constituent states. The governments that negotiated the Treaties of Rome, however, agreed upon an almost upside-down assignment of competences in which the "high politics" of foreign policy, public order, and defense was left to the member states while the "low politics" of economic regulation, commerce, and trade was to be transferred to Brussels. Pursuit of the supposedly "technical" goal of replacing the diversity of national regulations by uniform provisions in sector after sector led to a proliferation of committees, attempting to negotiate common regulations that reconciled often deeply held differences in national assumptions and local practices. The outcome was a mass of detailed regulations and directives, emerging out of a disjointed Brussels process that appeared to outsiders to pursue petty harmonization with enthusiasm while failing (because it lacked the capacity and authority) to tackle broader issues. The weakness of the functional approach to integration is its disaggregation of policymaking, with "technical experts" negotiating on separate dossiers without taking the broader political context into account.

Four interconnecting strategies have been followed in attempting to redistribute competences among this multilevel system of government and to contain the proliferation of detailed separate negotiations: mutual recognition, package deals, treaty revision, and development of the principle of subsidiarity. The crucial ECJ *Cassis de Dijon* ruling (1979) cut back the Sisyphean enterprise of detailed harmonization by encouraging a shift toward mutual recognition of national regulations and standards.[13] The 1992 Program built on this shift, assembling some three hundred market-opening negotiations into a package that raised their political visibility, increased pressures on governments to override entrenched interests, and so made it easier to make concessions in some sectors with some confidence that there would be compensating gains in others. [14]

Disentangling the political from the technical in such an opaque policy process—without an effective parliament or congress to alert participants to changing political sensitivities—is hard to achieve. National coordinating mechanisms struggle to impose priorities on the flow of paper; commissioners and their cabinets use their political judgment to mediate between the Commission services and the national political contexts with which they maintain contact. On one renowned occasion in 1973, an agricultural management committee struggling with the problem of the Community's mounting butter surplus agreed to dispose of a huge quantity to the Soviet Union, without stopping to consider the heightened political sensitivities involved or the likely backlash, at a time when EC butter prices were rising sharply in the three states which had just joined the EC, against the discovery that Russians were to be allowed to buy so much so cheaply.

Multilateral bargaining on multiple issues within the Community framework has therefore come to depend on the intermittent assembly of package deals, in which member governments make complex trade-offs across different dossiers and issue areas, enabling each to claim that it has made net gains on its specific priorities. But package deals require the investment of much political attention and prestige; they constitute exceptional interventions in the regular pattern of disaggregrated negotiations. At the broadest level, the constitutional and political framework itself can be reassessed and renegotiated, as in the IGCs that resulted in the Single European Act and the Maastricht Treaty. But these involve even greater investments of political

13. *Rowe-Zentral AG* v. *Bundesmonopolverwaltung für Branntwein*, Case 120/78, ECR 649, 1979.

14. Pelkmans, Winters, and Wallace (1988).

credit by heads of government, on both the European and the national levels. They reopen national debates about sovereignty and identity and European debates about political balance and underlying objectives. The increasingly frequent resort to this mechanism, with the third IGC in ten years anticipated for 1996, demonstrates the difficulties of holding to a stable institutional bargain between sovereignty and federation when the issues to be managed strike so deeply into the body of the nation-state.

The concept of subsidiarity came into the formal Community lexicon as the outcome of two separate developments: protests by the governments of the German *Länder* against the shift in the balance of policymaking authority within Germany resulting from Community intervention, and bitter opposition by the British government to use of the term *federal* (the F word, as those around Prime Minister Margaret Thatcher called it). The concept had its most relevant roots in Catholic social doctrine, with its teaching on the appropriate distribution of responsibilities among individual, family, local community, and state within a just social order. The principle expounded by Pope Pius XI in his 1931 encyclical, *Quadragesimo Anno,* which set out the Catholic critique of the Fascist state, was that "it is an injustice, a grave evil and a disturbance of right order for a larger and higher association to arrogate to itself functions which can be performed efficiently by smaller and lower societies."[15]

Translated from theological into constitutional language, this position will be familiar to students of federal constitutions as being close to that enunciated in the Tenth Amendment to the U.S. Constitution, or in article 30 of the Federal German *Grundgesetz.*[16] Sufficiently imprecise to meet the conflicting objectives of the British, of German state governments, and of others, it was incorporated into the Maastricht Treaty on European Union (article 3b), stating that

> In areas which do not fall within its exclusive competence, the Community shall take action, in accordance with the principle of

15. Pope Pius XI, *Quadragesimo Anno* (London, Catholic Truth Society, 1936), p. 31.

16. "The powers not delegated to the United States by the Constitution, nor prohibited by it to the States, are reserved to the States respectively, or to the people" (Tenth Amendment, U.S. Constitution). "The exercise of governmental powers and the discharge of governmental functions shall be incumbent on the *Länder* insofar as this Basic Law does not otherwise prescribe or permit" (article 30, Basic Law of the German Federal Republic). See Wilke and Wallace (1990); European Institute of Public Administration (1991).

subsidiarity, only if and in so far as the objectives of the proposed action cannot be sufficiently achieved by the Member States and can therefore, by reason of the scale or effects of the proposed action, be better achieved by the Community.

Any action by the Community shall not go beyond what is necessary to achieve the objectives of this Treaty.[17]

British negotiators, with little experience or understanding of the politics and law of multilevel government, entertained hopes that this new clause might provide a firm basis for legal challenges to Community proposals in new areas. German negotiators, familiar with the problems of managing constitutional federations, saw it more modestly as a useful symbolic declaration and point of reference for future bargaining.

British and French government attempts to "repatriate" legislation in 1992–93, in line with the spirit of this subsidiarity clause, came up against the same complexities of multilevel politics that had pushed so many rulemaking processes up to the Community level. Of the seventy-one items that Britain had listed for repatriation, only twenty-two survived for the consideration of the Brussels European Council, of which some sixteen were finally approved to be returned to national jurisdiction.[18] The inclusion of controls on pollution standards for drinking and bathing water—attempting to reverse EC directives agreed upon nearly twenty years before—was a victory for governments and affected industries in countries that fell short, but a defeat for environmental groups that looked to the Community as a source of support against their national governments. It was also a defeat for chemical companies in the Rhine Valley, which argued that the looser pollution controls imposed on their competitors in Britain constituted a distortion of competitive conditions within the single market.

The Commission's attempt, with the support of the French government, to apply the subsidiarity principle to the hunting of wild birds, in a draft directive presented to the European Parliament in April 1994, provoked intensive lobbying by environmental and conservation organizations. Hunting is, from one perspective, a matter for local regulation, but migratory birds cross national frontiers. Even

17. European Community, *Treaty of European Union* (Luxembourg, Office for Official Publications of the EC, 1992), article 3b, p. 18.

18. David Gardner, "More Retreat than Defeat on Euro-laws," *Financial Times,* December 13, 1993.

with respect to nonmigratory birds, environmentalists saw no reason to accept the premise that member governments of the EU should be allowed to fall below what they regarded as minimum standards for responsible democracies. The proposed directive thus ran into a highly political struggle over which principle—subsidiarity or environmental protection—should govern the treatment of this case, in which organizations from skeptical Britain were promoting the case for stronger Community powers against bodies from "integrationist" France.

Interest groups and campaigning organizations naturally tend to play one level of government off against each other to their best advantage, without observing abstract principles too closely. Application of the subsidiarity principle thus turns on politics and passion as much as on reason. The question of whether "traditional" Norwegian whaling practices came under the heading of national culture or Community fishing regulations was hotly contested in the context of accession negotiations in 1993–94, with similar difficulties in finding an objective basis on which to classify the issue. Completion of the EFTA enlargement negotiations added substantially to the Community's catalogue of endangered species, and to the list of treasured landscapes, around which future battles about appropriate jurisdiction and conflicting economic and environmental priorities might take place.

Acceptance of mutual recognition rather than insisting on negotiated harmonization, and of decentralized implementation rather than direct regulation, depends upon a sufficient degree of mutual respect and trust among Community governments, together with an acceptance of an underlying community of interest and values. Governments must be willing to accept the reliability of other countries' testing procedures as well as their formal standards and to accept also that standards will be applied and tests properly conducted.[19] The lesser the trust, the heavier the dependence on hard bargaining, detailed rules, and explicit harmonization; the greater the trust, the greater the tolerance of diversities of practice. Negotiation at the

19. Controversy erupted in Spain in late 1993 when a child was blinded by a toy imported from Taiwan. It had been imported into the EC through Rotterdam. The Dutch, it was alleged, had not tested the consignment because it was not destined for the Dutch market; but the Spanish authorities had, as a matter of standard practice, allowed the toys to enter untested since they had been sent on to Spain from another state within the single European market.

Community level of rules that within the United States are left to the discretion of individual states reflects this weaker sense of shared values, mutual trust, and common interest. The paradox of the subsidiarity debate within the EC is rooted in the fact that it developed as a substitute for addressing an explicitly federal agenda. Yet the evolution of the arguments that have surrounded it—over social policy and employment, and environmental regulation—has suggested that it is easier to accept the mutual recognition of state-made rules and the decentralized implementation of Community rules within a clearly political system of federal character than within the current uncertain compromise that the EC after Maastricht represents.

The development of regional policy, with financial transfers from the Community budget to regional and local authorities, has opened up a further dimension to this confederal system. The Commission and subnational authorities are natural allies against national governments—each seeking to use the others to bolster their position in the continuous struggle over the allocation of power and resources among different levels. The German *Länder* maintain their own offices in Brussels and are active both in the Bundestag in resisting the encroachment on federal competences through the evolution of Community negotiations and in Brussels in direct links with Commission services on regional, industrial, educational, and agricultural issues. In the course of the 1980s almost every local authority within Britain developed its own Community unit, focused on identifying Community spending programs that might benefit its locality and improving its chances of sharing in them—thus loosening British treasury control over local spending. Development of Community budgetary lines on education and research has had a similar impact on universities and institutes, with specialized offices and regular contacts with Brussels supplementing national links.

The outcome of this intricate and disaggregated pattern of politics is a policymaking process characterized by, to use the Euro-term, *lourdeur:* inertia, resistance to changes of direction, compartmentalized policymaking. It is a process particularly resistant to linkages between internal bargains and external negotiations—between, for instance, the commitment to assist economic and political transition in the former socialist countries and the ability of either the Commission or member governments to override the sectional interests of steelmakers, textile producers, and, above all, farmers and food processors in negotiating the Europe Agreements.[20]

The Sovereignty Block and the Problem of National Identity

Economic logic and technological advance have now significantly weakened the West European nation-state. However, political logic, within a region built upon the twin pillars of open market economies and democratic institutions, requires authoritative decisionmaking to be supported by a sense of shared political community much stronger than that which has as yet grown up within the European Community. The United States, a self-conscious "new nation," was able to mold its diverse citizens into a political community partly because they *were* all new, immigrants who had chosen to start again in a new world, and partly because, like its counterparts in nineteenth- and early twentieth-century Europe, it was equipped with all the instruments needed to shape national consciousness. These included a national education system designed to promote national values; a deliberately-promoted national myth; symbolic reinforcement of national history through national monuments, holidays, and the flag; widespread experience of national military service, including foreign wars; and a focus for national politics in Washington that commanded both substantial resources to distribute and substantial power to enforce national standards (including such psychological standards as the alleged boundaries between "American" and "un-American" activities).

Western Europe as a regional political system has access to few of these instruments, beyond the weak elements of community-building represented by university exchange programs and town-twinning schemes. Its citizens have become more familiar with each other as cross-border interactions have promoted a degree of social integration. Political rhetoric and historical experience, living together in

---

20. The ability of small sectional interests—raspberry growers, sausage producers—to defend their interests against pressures for adjustment was sharply displayed in these negotiations. After the conclusion of the Europe Agreement negotiations one weary Commission official (from DG-1, the External Relations Directorate-General) commented in a personal interview that he "had never before realized how important mushroom-growing was to the European Community."

"the West" self-defined in opposition to "the East," has reinforced an underlying sense of shared values.

But the weakness of central institutions, and of European political leadership, leaves interpretation and exploitation of these values without authoritative direction. Those who appeal to "European" values in deliberate contradistinction to the values of non-European cultures—Muslim, Confucian, even, for some, Californian—are to be found most often on the political right, promoting an idea of Europe that would close its borders against the trends of global economic and social integration. Attempts to provide an agreed upon version of European history rapidly run up against the fault lines of national historical experiences, with French perceptions of European history clashing with German, Hungarian with Portuguese, Western Catholic with Eastern Orthodox.[21] Effective promotion of a "new" European identity would require deliberate imposition of an authorized version: an impossible task without a good many of the real and symbolic resources of a federal state.[22]

Deep integration penetrates to the heart of national sovereignty. The Maastricht Treaty contained within its densely drafted clauses references to currency, taxation, and redistribution; law, judicial practice, policing, and border control; citizenship, representation, and education; and foreign policy and defense—the core functions of the traditional model of the nation-state, although presented here without the symbols of nationhood and statehood that bound together the traditional model. Attempts to roll back the penetration of national sovereignty by the spread of Community legislation have, as we have seen, come up against the logic of common action in policy areas in which territorial boundaries no longer fit economic, social, or security

21. Duroselle (1990) was the outcome of an attempt to define a broadly accepted version of European history. Written by a distinguished French historian, with an advisory committee of equally distinguished British, German, Italian, and Spanish historians, it was funded by the Bertelsmann Foundation and the European Commission and dedicated to Jean Monnet. It was sharply attacked on publication by Greeks within the EC and Slavic countries outside it for its bias toward a "Western Christendom" view. The reader is invited to imagine the operation and outcome of a Canadian-Mexican-American project to write a mutually acceptable history of North America, or a joint Japanese-Chinese-Korean committee to write a mutually acceptable history of East Asia; brief contemplation suggests that disagreements within Europe are modest by comparison.

22. Judt (1992) notes the particular sensitivity of reaching agreement on an interpretation of European history and identity for the past half century, in the aftermath of the end of the cold war.

interactions. While his French and British counterparts were carefully noting the limits placed on Community initiatives in the December 1993 Brussels European Council, German Chancellor Helmut Kohl was promising to place the transfer of further powers to the fledgling European Police Authority (Europol) among the highest priorities of his country's term of office in the Council presidency in the second semester of 1994. "The need for intense co-operation between governments is urgent," he argued, as a necessary response to the spread of organized crime across the EU. But common policing requires common rules on civil liberties and legal redress, and mechanisms of accountability to counterbalance the exercise of police powers Europe-wide—neither of which is as yet spelled out within the Maastricht Treaty.[23]

National identity depends upon shared myths and symbols, upon stability, security and familiarity. Market integration and technological advances bring change; personal, local community, and national political instability; and social transformation. The integration of Europe has weakened many of the symbols of national identity without supplying European symbols to take their place. National companies, and national technical advances, were sources of pride for European states a generation or two ago. National borders, guarded and flagged, marked the national territory. National media carried national news; radio and, in the early stages of its development, also television brought familiar voices in the national language operating within a shared national culture.[24] European nation-states created myths of ethnic homogeneity (despite the immense ethnic diversities they included); their fellow citizens were felt to be their kith and kin, members of the broader national family. National foreign policies represented and promoted the nation's place in the world, expressed its national character, and distinguished its national interests from those of its rivals and potential enemies.[25]

23. Quoted in Andrew Hill, "Kohl Plans to Take Europol Under His Wing," *Financial Times*, December 13, 1993, p. 3. The Spanish block at this European Council of approval of common Community rules on political asylum (necessary to implement common rules on entry into the Community from third countries), in view of the Belgian government's reluctance to extradite two Basques suspected of links with the separatist group Euzkadi ta Azkatasuna (Basque Nation and Liberty) also illustrates how deep into the fabric of each other's domestic order the spillover of rules has carried the Community.

24. Schlesinger (1991).

25. Anthony D. Smith (1991, 1992); Garcia (1993); William Wallace (1991b).

Cross-border takeovers, leading to the emergence of European or global companies, are economically rational and necessary to compete in wider markets. Machine-readable standardized passports make it possible to keep abreast of the explosion of people crossing Europe's external borders. Controls at internal borders have yielded to the weight of goods and numbers of people crossing them. Rising levels of migration, first from southern Europe, then from further south and east, have shaken the sense of shared ethnic and cultural community. Electronic media, with cable and satellite television, provide a far wider choice of information and entertainment—but the homogenized, internationalized, Americanized style buries the old familiar reference points of national values and eccentricities. Technical, economic, and social change brings with it a sense of threatened identity, of lost community—a sense most easily projected onto the European Community, as the apparent political force for change, the symbol of these threats, although not in reality their principal source. European elites, the successful or the advantaged who have benefited most from economic integration and the increased spatial and social mobility that it has brought, are least concerned about weakened identity at the national level. Mass publics, their jobs swept away or threatened by international competition and open borders, their towns and cities transformed by international companies and immigration, are—with some reason—far less convinced that the benefits of further integration outweigh the costs.

At the same time the existence of a broader economic, political and security Community loosens the ties that held nation-states together. The interdependence of national economies has been replaced by their integration into a wider regional economy. Mutual support against external threats to the national territory is no longer needed when the creation of a wider political Community has removed the threat. The balance of costs and benefits has shifted—and lowered the tolerance of richer regions within a single state for subsidies to their poorer regions. Thus Flanders resists the redistribution of Belgian taxes to Wallonia, and the Northern League in Italy has campaigned against subsidies to Rome and the south. Catalonia pursues prosperity as a European region rather than through the mediation of the Spanish state. Scots question whether their best interests are represented in Brussels by an English-dominated government, when Scottish prosperity depends upon Japanese and American companies producing for the European market and Scandinavian companies internationalizing their activities within the European framework. British and Irish governments negotiate on the contested future of Northern Ireland in the margins of European Council meetings.

Yet despite this weakening, the nation-state remains the basis for political identity and political accountability. No European leaders have emerged speaking a political language that the voters of different countries can understand. The European Parliament has so far remained a distant body seen largely through the mediation of national politics; the nonelected European Commission has only marginal popular legitimacy. Governments are still held to account by their electorates for policies over which they have less and less control, for economic success or failure that depends more and more upon the action of others and the success or failure of policy coordination. The responsibilities of government quickly teach ministers the limits to national autonomy and the logic of joint policies; but the dynamics of opposition and the groundswell of public unease encourage those outside government to demand that limits to integration be set.

From this contradiction has followed an underlying crisis of national politics and national identity across Western Europe, outside the Community as well as within, taking distinctive shapes in different countries, but with common roots in the weakening of the territorial basis for economics, social interaction, order, and security. Popular reactions against the Maastricht Treaty demonstrated the tensions in country after country. Analysis of the French referendum vote showed a majority for ratification in all the economically dynamic regions of France, and a majority against it in all those départements in decline. The first Danish referendum showed a large majority of women and public sector workers against the treaty, fearing a weakening of the national welfare system and the state structures that support it.[26] Press and opinion poll data in unified Germany demonstrated vigorous resistance to the prospect of "losing" the deutsch mark in the proposed monetary union: the symbol of national recovery and national strength for a country deprived of other reference points since World War II. The Swiss referendum on the European Economic Area agreement in December 1992 showed a sharp split between French and German cantons: the former relaxed about further integration

26. Kelstrup (1992).

into a Community that they identified with France, the latter resistant to the blurring of a national identity that had been created in opposition first to the Hapsburgs and later to Germany.

The European experience suggests that there are immense difficulties in building a political community on a broader level than the nation-state that will be sufficiently strong to support the strains and pressures of deep integration. A partial political community *has* developed in Western Europe: a security community within which established perceptions of physical threat have disappeared, an economic community strong enough to support a degree of redistribution, a politico-legal community firm enough for EC rules to be accepted and implemented. No such community has developed in any other international region. It has been a major achievement of the process of formal integration within Western Europe to have created such a community and to have widened it to include almost all the states of the Organization for European Economic Cooperation (or the Council of Europe). But the experience of the last decade in Europe, with a surge forward in formal integration and in informal interactions followed by widespread popular resistance, suggests that there are indeed limits to integration. These are set by the boundaries of sovereignty, identity, and accountability and will only be overcome— if they *can* be overcome—by qualitative and structural change, not by the gradual processes of multilateral rulemaking and regime-building within an increasingly opaque and complex treaty-based framework.

Chapter 5

European Integration, Global Integration

*T*HERE was, as noted in chapter 2, an intrinsic link between West
European integration and "global" integration in the immediate
postwar years. Integration within Western Europe was also integration
into "the West," under American leadership. European union, in the
eyes of the State Department, the Economic Cooperation Administration, and the defense and intelligence agencies that supported it,
was to reshape Western Europe on the American model and to equip
it to play a new role in an American-led international community.
Modernization within Western Europe was also, to an extent now
largely forgotten, also Americanization, entailing the adoption of American managerial practices, emulation of technology and production
patterns, openness to American investment, and admiration and imitation of American culture and social and political values.

West European integration was thus contained within Western
integration: a process of "civilian" economic and political integration,
within a broader security, political, and economic framework.[1] There
was, however, as has also been noted, an underlying tension from the
outset—between West European dreams of regained autonomy as a
"third force" and American assumptions about shared values and
acceptance of American leadership. This regional global tension sank
from sight in the early 1950s, in the face of an apparently clear and
present danger from the Soviet Union, to resurface again with the
relaxation of East-West relations in the late 1950s, the establishment
of the European Economic Community (EEC), the replacement of

1. Grosser (1980); Bull (1982).

87

the structural dollar surplus (after the recovery of West European economies) with a transatlantic dollar deficit, and the rebuilding of West European military capabilities.

The Kennedy administration's attempt to reconcile these two groupings took shape in 1961–62 in the concepts of the Atlantic Community, the Atlantic Partnership, and the "two pillars" supporting that partnership. British accession to the EEC was to be accompanied by a shift in the balance of the partnership, with Western Europe now shouldering a greater share of its military and economic burdens in the common cause. As French President Charles de Gaulle and his successors protested, the implicit assumption behind these concepts was that a more united Europe would continue to follow America's lead while shouldering a larger share of America's burdens as well as its own.[2] It was characteristic of the self-confidence of American foreign policy in the early 1960s that the potential incompatibility of interests between an enlarged European Community (EC) and its American ally was scarcely considered. The prevailing assumption was that commitment to common Western values would lead West European governments to the same policy positions that the American administration had reached.[3] The idea of Atlantic partnership also assumed a united Europe structurally capable of responding to American demands in a coherent and timely way—a massive overestimation of the institutional capabilities of the infant EEC (only five years old at the time of President John F. Kennedy's July 1962 "Declaration of Interdependence" speech).

The EEC was not, however, the only institution that the Kennedy administration saw as shaping the new Atlantic Partnership. The North Atlantic Treaty Organization (NATO), under continuing American leadership but with some reorganization to allow for greater weight to be given to West European—and particularly German—influence, was to be the main vehicle for politico-military integration, among West Europeans as well as across the Atlantic. Economic cooperation was to be managed within a revived Organization for European Economic Cooperation (OEEC), enlarged to bring the Americans themselves (and the Canadians) into full membership.[4] Over the

2. Grosser (1980, chapter 7).
3. Cleveland (1966).
4. The negotiations in 1959–61 that led to the transformation of the OEEC into the OECD were also linked to the failure of the British and Nordic governments to achieve a

objections of West European governments, which viewed Japan as a developing country, the Americans also insisted on bringing their other dependent and democratized ally into the new Organization for Economic Cooperation and Development (OECD).

There was no understanding behind this strategy that an integrated global economy was to be built around a succession of similar regional groupings. The Western international economy in the early 1960s was focused on the North Atlantic region itself. The American assumption was that a partnership of relative equals could be created between the United States itself and this potentially united Western Europe. It was, it should be noted, to be a bilateral partnership rather than a multilateral community. Those who formulated U.S. policy toward Western Europe under the Kennedy administration, as under the Eisenhower administration, were veterans of World War II in Europe and its aftermath. They retained much of the idealism of the postwar period, the hopes that a United States of Europe could be built along the American model. They also retained the direct links to West European governments and political leaders that had been established in those earlier years: assured access to people who expected enlightened American leadership.

The United States retained a sufficiently hegemonic position—economically, politically, militarily, and culturally—in the non-Communist world in the early 1960s to be confident that its partners would accept its definition of global order and would fit their evolving patterns of regional integration into that definition. U.S. policymakers also assumed that they would retain the right to intervene in discussions of regional integration within Western Europe, to ensure that their junior partners followed overall Western policies. Politico-military issues were to be handled within the Atlantic, not the West European, institutional structure; economic integration was to be pursued within the framework of liberal economic principles established by the General Agreement on Tariffs and Trade (GATT), the International Monetary Fund (IMF), and the OEEC and OECD.

---

wider but looser European free trade area and the consequent split between the EC-Six and the European Free Trade Association Seven. The United States, under both the Eisenhower and Kennedy administrations, supported the EC-Six, and pressed the British government to shift its position. The U.S. approach to revision of the OEEC reflected the view "that it should intervene more directly than in the past to try to assemble the Western countries in a new organisation containing both the individual countries and the two nascent European trade groupings"; Palmer and others (1968, p. 422).

The Gaullist challenge to this world view was fundamental, asserting that both European interests and European values were distinct from those of the United States and that European integration was an alternative rather than a complement to Western globalism. With Britain firmly in the American camp, Federal Germany was the battleground over which French and American protagonists struggled. The Franco-German Elysée Treaty of January 1963 represented the high point of Gaullist advance. The Atlanticist preamble that the Bundestag added to the treaty in the process of ratification—setting political and security limits on Federal Germany's developing relationship with France—signaled the beginning of the French retreat. The outcome was a standoff, in which France withdrew from the integrated structure of NATO and Germany joined its newly-created Nuclear Planning Group. The linkage between West European integration and American-led globalism was clear to all. Divergence among French, German, Dutch, and British assumptions about Atlantic cooperation was thus a central factor in the loss of the first impetus toward European union in the mid-1960s, in which high hopes of building supranational institutions gave way to disillusion.

When the impetus for formal integration within Western Europe was regained in the early 1970s—with the first attempt at economic and monetary union; enlargement to bring in Britain, Ireland, and Denmark; and the development of European political cooperation (EPC)—the United States' position as Western hegemon was much less secure. The Vietnam War had severely damaged America's political prestige within Western Europe; the Watergate controversy was to damage it further. The crisis of August 1971, when the Nixon administration unilaterally suspended dollar convertibility, demonstrated both the extent to which America had lost the capacity to manage the global economy and the extent to which American policymakers were prepared to make decisions at the expense of European interests.

The Nixon administration's response, however, was very much in line with that of the Eisenhower and Kennedy administrations a decade and more before: to seek to reorder Atlantic institutions to ensure that West European integration continued to fit within a wider American-led framework. The style of the Nixon-Kissinger Year of Europe initiative of 1973 was more brutally Realist than that of the Kennedy initiative of 1962. There was much less emphasis on common aspirations and values, more on underlying power relations.

"The political, military and economic issues in Atlantic relations are linked by reality, not by our choice nor for the tactical purpose of trading one off against the other," Henry Kissinger declared in his Year of Europe speech of April 23, 1973. He made quite clear his determination to link European concessions on foreign policy and economic issues to acceptance of the primacy of American security provision—and therefore of American leadership. America, he argued, was a global power, whereas "Europe" was a regional power, which should by implication accept its ancillary role within an American-led global order.[5]

One item on the American agenda was a demand for American representatives to sit in on meetings within EPC to ensure that their discussions were compatible with consultations within the NATO framework. If the West Europeans were determined to insist on trespassing on the field of high politics, their American partners thought it entirely reasonable to act as stewards, to guide them along an acceptable path. The launching of an independent Euro-Arab dialogue at the December 1973 European Council, in the aftermath of the Gulf War and oil embargo, provoked outbursts of mutual denunciation between Washington and Paris. The Nixon administration exerted direct pressure on Bonn and London to give first priority to channeling negotiations with the Arab oil producers through the American-led International Energy Agency (IEA).[6]

The 1973–74 transatlantic confrontation was finally resolved within the context of the Ottawa NATO summit of June 1974. Both the terms of the reconciliation and the institutional framework within which it was celebrated underlined the overriding importance of the security link and the willingness of governments on both sides of the Atlantic to subordinate economic and political disputes to this wider common interest. The priority of the security link continued to obtain until the watershed of the 1989–91 revolutions, moderating disputes and imposing an overall political imperative on lower-level conflicts.

5. William Wallace (1976); Kissinger (1982, pp. 151–55).

6. William Wallace and Allen (1977); de Schoutheete (1986). Keohane (1984, chapter 10) considers the IEA as a transitional example of the establishment of a functional regime in a world moving away from U.S. hegemony; but the political pressures that accompanied its establishment demonstrated that, at least in 1973–74, the United States remained the hegemonic power within the Western alliance when it was prepared to use its security predominance to offset its relative economic decline. French ministers saw the establishment of the IEA as the successful reassertion of American hegemony.

The pattern of United States–Europe relations in the 1970s and 1980s was of the accommodation of divergent policies, the pursuit of competitive advantage, and the defense of specific interests. Agricultural disputes figured prominently throughout this period. First chickens, then cheese, then orange juice, then soya and corn gluten became political issues, preoccupying governments and filling newspaper headlines—proof of the concentrated lobbying power of agricultural interests more than the intrinsic importance of the trade at stake. Airline interests were another recurring source of friction, a field in which intergovernmental bargaining over allocation of routes and airport slots could be measured directly in market shares, profits won, and jobs created. The unexpected success of the Airbus consortium in holding its own in a field that American manufacturers were beginning to think of as a natural American monopoly aroused further second-order frictions.

West European concern to manage continued global cooperation with what seemed to European leaders a more distracted and self-centered United States led in the 1970s to European initiatives to establish new linking institutions. The idea of Western summits was an extension of the settled French preference for European summits; the institutionalization of European Councils was paralleled by the development of the Group of Seven (G-7). In the original Giscard-Schmidt conception, Western summitry was intended to provide West European governments with leverage over American policies, to compensate for the United States' sometimes absent-minded leverage over European policies.[7] The presence of four West European governments (Federal Germany, France, Britain, and Italy) among seven, together with the president of the Commission and on occasion the head of government of another member state as that semester's president of the Council made for a more advantageous balance than that which American proponents of Atlantic partnership had envisaged—but it did not guarantee greater influence for the individualist and independent-minded leaders of separate European states, presenting loosely coordinated proposals. Despite the (often passive) participation of Japan, G-7 summitry was thus primarily a transatlantic dialogue rather than a mechanism for managing an emerging trilateral world. G-7 itself began as a self-consciously "civilian" and

7. Putnam and Bayne (1987).

economic gathering. Politicomilitary issues were handled in the more restrictive G-4 grouping of the United States, France, Britain, and Germany—the central players within NATO.[8]

The implementation of coherent West European approaches to global—by which was meant Western, United States–led—cooperation and integration was complicated by the distinctive interests of the major West European governments. Britain remained much more a global investor and financial center than its neighbors, even though its visible trade had reoriented itself toward the European continent. It had a far higher level of inward and outward investment and a much lower level of state ownership of financial institutions, industrial companies, and services than any of its major continental partners— even before the large-scale privatizations of the 1980s. Federal Germany was the most regionally concentrated trader and the most regionally focused in terms of foreign and security interests. For economic and historical reasons, Germany thus had very few extra-European interests in comparision to France, Britain, and Italy. France was more explicitly mercantilist than either Britain or Germany, approaching the management of interdependence in terms of striking the hardest bargain that could be gained between the French state as sponsor of French industry and foreign public or private partners.

Globalizing trends in the developed world economy in the 1970s and 1980s made for more difficult national and European choices. French governments alternated between calls for explicit European strategies and negotiated bargains between French state companies and American partners with valuable technologies and access to U.S. markets to share. French and German resistance to Japanese penetration was punctuated by competition for Japanese investment or partnerships. Only the British government, which explicitly avoided either an industrial or a European strategy, was spared such intricate choices—at the cost, it seemed to its partners, both of following the shifts of American opinion too closely and of abandoning concern for national economic interests in favor of accepting Japanese and American revitalization of its decayed industrial base.

---

8. Protests from the Italians (and Dutch), and unease in Tokyo, about the exclusivity of the Guadeloupe four-power summit of January 1979, the agenda for which ranged from nuclear modernization in Europe to relations with China, began to break down this division between economic and political summitry. The Williamsburg summit of 1983 completed this integration of the political and economic agendas. See Putnam and Bayne (1987).

For much of this period transatlantic management of issues of standards and harmonization remained at the technical level, overshadowed by political disputes on burden sharing, nuclear weapon deployment, East-West relations, or agricultural trade. The well-established position of American companies in Europe enabled them not only to keep in close touch with European negotiations but often to take part in them. When the EC and major West European governments responded to fears about Japanese competitiveness in the early 1980s by developing collaborative programs in high technology, American companies with research and manufacturing bases in Europe managed, after applying some pressure, to gain access to them.[9] U.S. companies and their advisers in Brussels maintained an expert watch on Commission proposals and their progress and were quick to intervene with advice or with pressure on whichever member government was seen as most likely to be supportive. Quiet pressure on the U.S. mission to the EC to intervene represented the next stage up the ladder of deterrence; open appeals to Washington represented major escalation.

European grievances against the United States were more substantial. They focused on successive occasions on what were seen as U.S. attempts to use security arguments and regulation to gain competitive advantages in trade and economic regulation. Controls on East-West trade, especially in high technology, were a particular source of tension. European computer manufacturers accused the U.S. administration of passing on confidential information submitted to the surveillance committee on East-West trade of the NATO Coordinating Committee on Multilateral Export Controls. American use of controls on licenses extended by U.S. companies to block West European companies supplying pumping equipment for Soviet gas pipelines was seen—by the British Conservative government as well as by its partners—as unacceptable extraterritorial extension of U.S. jurisdiction.[10] The Reagan administration's invitation to West European companies to participate as subcontractors in the Strategic Defense Initiative was seen as a further attempt to strengthen American technological superiority through controls on European research and development. The Eureka program for European collaboration in advanced technology was the French-led West European response.[11]

    9. Sharp and Shearman (1987).
    10. Rosenthal and Knighton (1982).
    11. Sharp and Shearman (1987); Sandholtz (1992).

The 1992 Program was for West European governments a constructive exercise in deepening regional economic integration through the extension of mutual recognition and the harmonization of standards in a number of areas. The American response, as the program emerged into political visibility in 1987–88, was couched in terms of a threat; fears of a "Fortress Europe," creating its own standards in order to exclude American business, were whipped up by alarmist lobbies and press reports. The idea that a regional grouping in Western Europe might develop its own industrial standards and regulations without American participation was as difficult to accept as the idea that West European governments might cooperate on foreign policy without American participation.[12]

Transatlantic diplomacy, and the swing of American public concerns about competitiveness from Europe to Asia and back again, calmed the atmosphere in the course of 1989–90. But fears of an economically successful European Community mounting a challenge to American technological supremacy continued to rise and fall in and around Washington into the early 1990s. The image of a coherent and competitive Europe, deliberately developing market rules and research collaboration to the disadvantage of the United States, was an absurdly exaggerated portrayal of the hesitant progress of the EC toward deeper integration; but it supported a good many consultants and sold a lot of books in an intellectual climate preoccupied with lost hegemony and "American decline."[13] A generation that had assumed American economic as well as security leadership, defining the terms of economic cooperation and setting the standards for technological trade, appeared to find adjustment to the prospect of a more balanced partnership with a regionally integrated Western Europe difficult to accept.

The Complications of Post–Cold War Europe

The weakening, and potential disappearance, of the security and political framework that has for forty years contained West European

12. Woolcock (1992).

13. Thurow (1992) was one of the most authoritative of these alarmist studies. Its cover carried an EC flag, overshadowing the U.S. flag (*and* the Japanese flag), which in turn carried the flag of Federal Germany at its center. The image suggested that Germany was the powerhouse of the European economy and the focus for the European threat.

integration is therefore a radical shift. The basis for transatlantic relations, which have set the context for the reconciliation of regional and global priorities, altered sharply between 1989 and 1993. The number of American troops in Europe declined from 350,000 in mid-1989 to 100,000 in mid-1993; the numbers of Red Army troops in central Europe, the rationale for the Americans' presence in such strength, had declined even more rapidly, with the last contingents withdrawing beyond Poland's eastern border in August 1994. American impatience with the slow pace and self-absorption of European policymaking is no longer constrained by politico-military considerations. European impatience with the slow pace and self-absorption of Washington policymaking is no longer constrained by acceptance of the overriding importance of maintaining the U.S. military commitment.

The disappearance of the familiar boundaries of Western Europe was a radical development. A clearly defined region, the institutions of which contained a manageable number of members and associated states, opened into an ill-defined expanse, with a potential institutional membership of over thirty states—and with new states appearing out of the breakup of Yugoslavia, the Soviet Union, and Czechoslovakia. The European Commission had a unit of six *fonctionnaires* managing its relations with the socialist bloc at the beginning of 1989. Two years later it had several hundred, attempting to manage a range of new programs focussed upon these rapidly changing countries that were pressing first for association and then for full membership. The EC now found itself negotiating at once with their governments and with those interests within the existing Community positively or adversely affected by the transformation, training their new cadres to understand the intricacies of multilateral bargaining, the interaction between domestic law and international regulation, the distinctions between private and public interests, and the limitations of financial and economic autonomy in an open global economic order. The political objectives of European integration were emphasized by a lengthening queue of applicants asking for political commitment in the hope that economic concessions would follow.

Several central and extremely awkward questions about regional international integration, which it had been possible to an extent to sidestep during the cold war, have thus been posed anew. In a global economy in which no one state or region predominates, and in which institutional structures for regional integration differ significantly from region to region, who defines the rules for global economic cooperation and the balance between global and regional integration? What is the linkage, if any, among global economic cooperation, global military security, and global political order? How can participants agree to draw and hold the boundaries of regional integration from region to region—and what are the implications of such boundary drawing for those who are left outside and for the long-term stability of the global political and economic order?

Neither Western Europe nor the United States had to answer these questions in the forty years before 1989. The French government posed several of them in its challenge to American leadership in the early 1960s, even promoting the mental map of "Europe from the Atlantic to the Urals" in opposition to that of "the West." But the resistance of its German partner to French pressure, and the sharpness of the American response, pushed them back. Both the Americans and the West Europeans continued to assume throughout the 1970s and 1980s that in the last resort American preferences would prevail, and that shared security considerations would override divergent economic interests.

The relative decline of the United States' economic position shifted the balance of influence but did not overturn the established pattern. U.S. ambassadors to NATO and to the EC and officials and cabinet members from Washington continued to set the terms of acceptable West European regional integration. By and large West European governments continued to accept those terms and to work within them, thus avoiding the problem of negotiating among themselves their own definition of global economic cooperation, or of reconciling the different approaches the French, German, and British governments would wish to take. The United States continued to act as a global power, and West European states individually and collectively as a regional power, partly because the relationship suited both sides.[14] If Western Europe as an entity had attempted to play a more active global economic or political role, it would have needed stronger

14. Keohane (1984) and Nye (1990) give rather different explanations for this continuation of American predominance beyond the period of American economic hegemony. Keohane focuses on the importance of Western institutions in maintaining the assumptions that their American designers had built into them. Nye notes both the continuing importance of the security link and the influence of "soft power": of American ideas and American culture, widely diffused and absorbed throughout Western Europe (and East Asia).

collective institutions and greater capacities for regional political leadership, either from major governments (France, Germany, Britain) or from the Commission. Underlying differences between France and Germany—the core partnership for West European cooperation throughout the 1970s and 1980s—about European-American relations and about the links between institution-building within Western Europe and at the global and Western levels inhibited any such developments.

Despite the evolution of G-7 summitry and the rising importance of the regional East Asian economy, moreover, relations between the United States as global leader and the EC and its member states as regional partner continued to be managed bilaterally rather than multilaterally. Surges of interest in "trilateralism" and a gradual strengthening during the 1980s of political relations between Japan and Western Europe did not tip the balance toward multilateralism very far. Even such professedly multilateral negotiations as the GATT Uruguay Round were defined by the United States, and largely accepted by the EC, as first and foremost a transatlantic bilateral bargain, separated from bilateral American bargaining with East Asian countries, with the interests and obligations of other groups and countries as secondary.[15]

In the five years between the demolition of the Berlin Wall and the fall of 1994 neither the United States nor the European Union (EU) had managed to provide coherent answers to these underlying questions. The landscape around them was still too subject to aftershocks from that great earthquake for more than the erection of temporary structures on provisional sites. Russian troops were still on German soil, although they were due to complete their withdrawal in the summer of 1994. Russia itself was evidently unstable, within the even more unstable space of the former Soviet Union and its many successor states. Political and economic transition within the states of east-central and eastern Europe was incomplete. Russian tropps remained on German soil until the summer of 1994.

Above all the breakup of Yugoslavia had demonstrated the scale of the challenges posed to established patterns of regional integration and to attempts to maintain a separation among the economic, political, and security dimensions of regional order. In the spring of 1991

15. Paarlberg (1994) notes the importance of domestic American agricultural interests in shaping this bilateral approach to multilateral negotiation.

an EC committee was considering revision of the association agreement with Yugoslavia; the Greek representative's attempt to introduce the political question of relations between Serbia and Croatia into the discussions was resisted by others around the table. The working group of foreign ministry planners within EPC is reported to have prepared a joint paper on potential developments within Yugoslavia in the course of 1990, but it did not gain the attention of ministers. Disaggregated policymaking by governments preoccupied with negotiations within the pre-Maastricht intergovernmental conference and with the political and economic implications of the unification of Germany left them unprepared to cope with the interconnected security, political, and economic aspects of the Yugoslav crisis. They were unprepared, too, to cope with the withdrawal of American politico-military leadership, which was signaled by Washington as the crisis developed.

Institutions for regional integration are not equipped to manage military conflict. Economic cooperation and international regulation can be managed by committees, laboriously pursuing consensus through extended negotiation. Military action (like currency management) requires clear lines of authority and accountability, available only within statelike structures. The "failure" of the EU to manage successfully the developing Yugoslav conflict was embedded in the Community's ambiguous character as an economic organization with political objectives, and in the resulting gap between the rhetoric of European union and its institutional capacities. In one (often overlooked) respect the Community did demonstrate its strength and success over Yugoslavia. Apart from briefly held suspicions in the early months and from the emotional campaign in the winter of 1991 that led the German government to push its partners into early recognition of the independence of Croatia, this area—which had been the focus of great power rivalry among Germany, Italy, and France in repeated past conflicts—did not divide the states of Western Europe.[16] They held together; though they also, for the most part, held back.

16. This maintenance of solidarity, in spite of severe pressure from domestic lobbies, from disruption of transport routes, and from the disproportionate weight of refugees entering Germany and Italy, provides a conclusive answer to the gloomy realist prognostications of John Mearsheimer (1990). Institutions matter a great deal; elite socialization, even mass interaction, lessens misunderstanding and mutual suspicion among states under conditions of crisis.

None of the other, weaker, international organizations that were drawn into the Yugoslav conflict managed any better than the EU. The Conference on Security and Cooperation in Europe demonstrated its incapacity and incoherence within the first three months. NATO and the West European Union (WEU) were caught up for several months in an absurd duplication of naval patrols in the Adriatic—each commanded by different Italian admirals, neither with clear instructions, sailing symbolically up and down the Dalmatian coast. The United Nations provided legitimation for expanding peacekeeping, and "peace-making," operations but could provide only uncertain political direction to the military commanders on the ground. The most sobering lesson of three years of international involvement in the conflict in the former Yugoslavia is that the diffusion of authority and responsibility involved in institutionalized multilateral diplomacy, even when it is as intensely structured as EPC had become in twenty years of operation, encourage states to shuffle off hard choices onto each other; there is no place for the buck to stop beyond a statelike (or federal) structure.

Almost as sobering a lesson is that the disaggregated policy processes of institutionalized regional integration prevent an overall approach either to anticipation of crises or to management of their consequences. The EC was developing programs of economic and technical assistance to the former socialist states of southeastern Europe in 1990–91. The outbreak of the conflict in Yugoslavia disrupted the economies of neighboring states, most severely that of Bulgaria. Imposition of sanctions on Serbia, and their subsequent tightening on the Danube, extended the disruption the conflict had already created in the other Danube basin states, in Romania and Hungary as well as Bulgaria. But political and security policies were only loosely linked to economic programs; no special measures were taken to compensate these neighboring states for the damage to their fragile economies, leaving embittered governments decreasingly willing to assist in the enforcement of sanctions that appeared to set back their own hopes of recovery without persuading the Serbs to change policy.

American reactions to the transformation of Europe, and to the conflict in Yugoslavia, have similarly linked security, political, and economic aspects, without offering any clear redefinition of their preferred institutional framework for this enlarged region or for how it should fit into an Atlantic or global framework. After a year in office,

President Bill Clinton delivered his administration's first authoritative message to Western Europe, in the context of the NATO summit (and associated United States–European Union discussions) in Brussels on January 10–11, 1994. The signal (in his Brussels Town Hall speech on January 9, 1994) was one of partial disengagement: political support and intermittent political intervention, maintenance of a modest military presence, and expectation that Western Europe would carry the main burden of economic adjustment to the East:

> You have the most to gain from a Europe that is integrated in terms of security, in terms of economics, in terms of democracies.
>
> Ultimately you will have to decide what sort of Europe you want and how hard you are willing to work for it. But I want you to know that the United States stands by you in that battle, as we have in the other battles of the 20th century.[17]

These discussions among West European and North American heads of government ranged from the partial extension of NATO's boundaries further east, through the Partnership for Peace proposals, to "the imperative of helping to integrate the new market democracies of Europe's eastern half into the Transatlantic Community."[18] Economic integration, democratic consolidation, and security provision were thus all offered as linked parts of an overall Western response. Integration into the EU was at the same time to be integration into the wider "transatlantic Community," regional and global integration thus going together. However, American officials made clear, it was now up to the West Europeans to carry the largest share of the financial and economic burden of this American-led political commitment. The linkage between political leadership and financial burden was thus to be broken.[19]

What was the European "region" that was now to be the United States' partner? Was it the EU and NATO member states of Western Europe, partners with the United States in extending aid to Eastern

17. Agence Europe, "Bill Clinton's First Official Visit to Europe," *Europe Documents*, no. 1868, January 14, 1994, p. 7.

18. Agence Europe, "Bill Clinton's First Official Visit," p. 8.

19. American policymakers who expected their European allies to accept this division of political and financial responsibilities were evidently unconscious of the historical parallels. The American war of independence stemmed from the colonies' resistance to shouldering their share of the burden of British imperial defense without sharing equally in the direction of imperial policy.

Europe? Or was it now to become a larger Europe, stretching perhaps from the Atlantic almost to the Urals, nevertheless to be absorbed within an expanded Atlantic community? The political and institutional problems of enlargement—of the EU, the WEU, and NATO—were compounded by the immense difficulties and sensitivities of drawing any boundaries to this larger Europe's eastward extension, and of developing any mutually acceptable form of association with those countries that were to be left outside.

The European Community was committed by the terms of the Treaties of Rome to progressive enlargement. Article 238 of the treaty declares that "any European state may apply to become a member of the Community." In the cold war conditions of 1957, that was a limited commitment. In the years after 1989 it threatened to overwhelm the EC, as hopeful applicants declared their intentions and West European governments struggled to find ways to respond that conveyed neither a promise of early entry nor a threat of permanent exclusion. Problems of institutional balance, of economic and financial adjustment, of security provision, and of popular acceptability all flowed from substantial enlargement. Links between NATO and the WEU, and now the WEU and EU, made it impossible to treat EU enlargement and the extension of Western security guarantees as separate issues. Potential applicants in any event made it clear that they were looking at once for economic assistance and access and for multilateral security.

Unification of Germany had transformed the immediate economic balance of the Community and the long-term political balance of Europe. Disintegration of the Soviet Union had redrawn the map of Eastern Europe and opened the prospect that at least some of its constituent republics might hope to follow the path that the east-central European states were already taking and "join the West." Russia and Ukraine (like Turkey) were agreed by all to be too large, too distant, too unstable, and too poor to be conceivable candidates for EU membership. But that left difficult decisions to be made about the prospect of membership to be offered to the smaller countries between the EU and the western boundaries of these three large Eurasian states, and about the development of patterns of association that could satisfy their needs without overloading the EU. To the south, the states of the southern Mediterranean with their rapidly rising populations were actively concerned about the diversion of trade, investment flows and financial assistance toward Eastern Europe. The EU could not ignore the potential political and security consequences of such a diversion. Western Europe's response to the emergence of this larger region could not be delivered in economic terms alone, nor justified to its reluctant electorates primarily in terms of economic benefits. The scale of the economic transformation involved, and its importance for the future balance of the global economy and political order, made it essential to bring together any strategy to build a larger European region within a wider concerted strategy for linked regional and global integration. But there was, in the fall of 1994, no West European strategy and no effective global forum within which to develop a wider concerted strategy.[20]

This discussion has taken the chapter some way beyond the politics of deep integration among the advanced industrial democracies. But the global economy is not easily divisible into definable regions of comparable countries, neat building blocks for global integration. The boundaries of the West European economy were defined by political and military factors in the forty years before 1989, not by any natural or permanent geoeconomic factors. International regions are mental constructs: the stuff of geopolitics, not of economic development alone. Whether Russia or Turkey belongs in a framework for regional integration with Germany, France, and Britain is as subjective a question as whether China or Indonesia belongs in a regional framework with the United States. The choice must be made in terms of first political, and second economic objectives: of which countries are seen as most suitable and acceptable partners and of which area is seen to form the most natural region for collective economic management.

Any regional organization faces a choice of priorities between width and depth: between the greater coherence, solidarity, and exclusiveness of a smaller, tighter grouping and the greater incoherence,

20. Alasdair Smith and Wallace (1994). Enlargement raises awkward questions for the North American Free Trade Agreement and Asian-Pacific Economic Cooperation (APEC), of course, as well as for the EU. The APEC Eminent Persons report argues "that it will be increasingly difficult to realize the ambitious expansion of APEC's functions . . . if the membership of the organization were to be increased substantially in the near future. . . . We therefore counsel caution in augmenting the membership." Asia-Pacific Economic Cooperation (1993 p. 59).

diversity, and openness of a wider regional entity. The intensity of formal integration, the institutional strength and administrative obligations that have grown up in Western Europe make the choice of priorities for the EU particularly delicate. Few within the current member states are prepared to jeopardize what has been achieved by admitting new members that lack the domestic framework of efficient administration, formulation and implementation of laws and regulations, transparency of market transactions, and access to the courts by private actors in search of redress that are necessary for mutual trust within a deeply integrated community. But none is willing to brush aside the political imperatives that press enlargement toward the East onto a reluctant Western Europe.

The Overloaded Agenda: Regional Integration as a Distraction from Global Integration

Even under stable conditions, policymaking within such a weak confederal structure is characteristically slow and tortuous. The conditions for multilateral and multilevel bargaining on a complex agenda among largely autonomous governments impose unavoidable delays. Domestic opponents have to be reconciled or bought off; concessions have to be traded among the major players; side payments have to be negotiated with the minor players. Where there are, in addition, external interests to be considered, deliverable packages are even harder to assemble. There is an understandable tendency to leave external considerations to last, to expect others to recognize the imperatives of internal politics while declining to recognize that other countries face imperatives of their own.

Such a tendency will be familiar to students of U.S. trade policy before World War II—and not unfamiliar to students of U.S. trade policy and congressional politics today. Once internal bargains have been struck it is hard to undo them; external negotiations then proceed on the basis of the assumptions that have been set, in the expectation that others will accept them too. The GATT Uruguay Round offered the cautionary spectacle of a federal system negotiating with a confederal one. The delays endemic to such political systems compounded each other, with each side calling on the other to see the issues on the table "our way."[21] The interests of third countries, the large majority of GATT members, were thus squeezed to the margins of this officially multilateral negotiation.

The experience of negotiating the Europe Agreements with central and East European states confirms the lessons derived from the management of common commercial policy through successive GATT rounds. Compartmentalized policy coalitions successfully resisted attempts to override them on broader political grounds; entrenched lobbies intervened at the national and the Community level, with agricultural ministers competing in championing what they claim to be national interests against concessions to Polish and Hungarian farmers and food processors.

The experience of negotiating the constitutional and policy package encapsulated in the intergovernmental conferences of 1991 is even more striking. Preoccupation, at all levels of government, with the negotiations, with the building of coalitions and the launching of initiatives, with the management of domestic opinion and the presentation of preferred outcomes to domestic and foreign audiences, unavoidably left less time and attention for other issues. The question of future enlargement of the Community was explicitly left off the agenda as too complex to include within the package and capable of being postponed to a later date. Relations with Eastern Europe and with the disintegrating Soviet Union intruded. So, more painfully, did the outbreak of conflict within Yugoslavia. So did the slow progress of negotiations within the Uruguay Round. The parallel negotiations within NATO on a new alliance strategy were directly linked to the foreign and security title of the proposed treaty and were therefore effectively integrated into the Maastricht round. But the EC's halting

21. The intricacy of the multilevel games played in such an interfederal negotiation is far more complex than is suggested in the concept of "two-level games." American companies with interests at stake in the Uruguay Round, for instance, lobbied not only their own federal government but also, where advantageous, the EC Commission and the ministries of EC member states that participated in bargaining over EC positions. Some also developed links with the European Parliament as well as Congress; others were assiduous in informing European media of potential costs and benefits, particularly where they had employees within the country (or even electoral district) concerned. Some European companies are learning to be as active in Washington and beyond. Those engaged follow each other's written and broadcast media, feeding back into the game messages intended for the ears of others. Hardly surprisingly the skills required to play this multilevel, multiple-actor game successfully are beyond many governments. See Evans, Jacobson, and Putnam (1993).

response to the transformation of central and Eastern Europe was partly the result of the crowding out of attention to East European issues by the time spent on the complicated internal politics of Western Europe.

West European integration was initiated with the help of an external sponsor and hegemon. Its growth was eased by the continuing external provision of security and political leadership, resolving the dilemma of reconciling French, German, and British pretensions to leadership within the region by mutual acceptance of American leadership instead. The problem of regional leadership and of the reemergence of a regional hegemon is posed by the reunification of Germany and the reorientation of a wider Europe around Germany. The Franco-German partnership has served until now as a substitute form of regional leadership: a dual hegemony based upon mutual need and mutual uncertainty, and on shared recognition of the unacceptability of German regional leadership. On economic issues within the scope of the treaties, the European Commission itself under a politically skillful president can provide some of the elements of leadership, setting the agenda for member governments, although dependent on the creation of coalitions among member governments for decisionmaking and implementation. Collective, dispersed leadership of regional structures is unavoidably heavy and cumbersome; it is slow and reactive and approaches the reconciliation of regional and global priorities most often on the basis of compromises already struck and differences of view carefully papered over.

The prospect of a world economy managed by multilateral bargaining among several such organized groupings, in which the negotiating position of each grouping has been constructed out of careful compromises among its large and small member states, is not a confident recipe for global integration. In such a regionally organized global economic structure it would be prudent to assume that other regional groups would have weaker institutional structures than the EU, less able to address the awkward trade-offs among political, economic, and security considerations that arise even in primarily economic multilateral negotiation. Those states that were left outside such regional groups would be marginalized in international economic negotiations, unless they were able to assemble effective bargaining coalitions in their turn.

In the Western international economy over the past forty-five years it has been the United States that has set the agenda and provided the resources and the market access needed to hold the system together. In the trilaterally organized world economy envisaged in the early 1980s, it could safely be assumed that the United States would continue to hold the three regional economies together, because of its political and security commitment to Western Europe and to East Asia. In the transformed security environment of the 1990s the political and security binding that has held these three regions together is much less strong—and the willingness of the American public to provide the resources to maintain it is in doubt. A "three circles" image, in which the United States continues to carry influence over the evolution of European integration while at the same time playing a leading role in regional integration in the Western Hemisphere and in the Asia-Pacific region, is a beguiling prospect.[22] It is unlikely, however, to appeal to the members of other regional organizations, any more than would a pattern of economic cooperation centered on bilateral bargaining with the United States.[23]

A shift from American global leadership toward shared economic management is a necessity in the post–cold war environment. There is, however, little to be learned from the experience of West European economic integration during the cold war years and its relations with the United States and United States–led global institutions that will help us to understand what is needed to reconcile global and regional integration in a post–cold war world. We will have to develop the rules for this new global order without searching for historical parallels—as those who created the institutions of regional integration in Western Europe did in their time.

22. The three circles concept was developed by British foreign office planners during World War II. Taken up by Winston Churchill, it became the governing concept for British foreign policy for over thirty years after 1945. The imagery was of a Britain that compensated for the decline in independent resources by exercising guiding influence in three distinctive networks: the "special relationship" with the United States, the British Commonwealth and Empire, and the alliance with continental Western Europe. As a concept it had immense appeal within the British political establishment, but it was not widely appreciated or understood in other countries—even in the United States.

23. Alongside the optimists within the United States who look for a cooperative relationship among these United States–sponsored regional groups are pessimists who fear a destructive rivalry among three competing industrial blocs; see Thurow (1992).

Comments

Suzanne Berger

Are globalization of economic activities and international agreements on harmonization of domestic practices and institutions reshaping nation states? Do the experiences of the West Europeans, engaged over the past four decades in a deliberate process of regional institution-building, offer any lessons about how to bring about deep integration, or about its desirability? William Wallace addresses these issues in a wide-ranging and thoughtful history of the evolution of the European Union (EU) from the early postwar years to the present. Europe provides the strongest single case of long-established sovereign states attempting in parallel to regulate economic exchanges by market-opening and to govern the interactions of their societies and economies with common rules and institutions. It is therefore of special interest in any analysis of the prospects for deep integration in the world economy.

Wallace is skeptical about the lessons that the rest of the world might draw from the EU and throughout the volume he stresses the specificity of European circumstances. Three facts make this experience essentially unique, in Wallace's view: the creation of an institutional framework—a virtual constitutional order—forty years before the region had to confront the challenges of deep economic interdependence and globalization; the political objectives at stake in establishing these institutions in the immediate postwar period; and

Suzanne Berger is Ford International Professor of Political Science at the Massachusetts Institute of Technology.

finally the degree of interpenetration of national life by crisscrossing elite networks centered on Brussels.

Wallace's doubts about the relevance of Europe for understanding the future of deep integration elsewhere in the world seem above all to focus on this last point: on the centrality to the integration process of elite networks and elite learning over repeated rounds of joint problem-solving. In no other parts of the world do the political or bureaucratic elites of different nations share anything like the long trajectory of common experiences and decisionmaking that has been traversed together by the main policymakers of the European Community (EC), writes Wallace. This dense and resilient network of elite interactions explains the success and forward movement of the EU. Even though Wallace points to the overwhelming importance of politics in the founding of the Community, it thereafter seems to vanish from the scene. In his account politics seems to figure primarily as a lag factor, as a drag. The theme that runs through the work is the contradiction between political logic, which operates to preserve national sovereignty, and economic logic and technological advance, which work for regional integration. Forward momentum in constructing the Community has depended on the force of economic interests and on the commitment of elites socialized by common experience.

Wallace makes a strong case for his reading of the European story, and one that, part by part, seems compelling. But considering the whole, the burden carried in his argument by elite networks, and secondarily by "economic logic and technological advance," seems very great indeed. There is another way of thinking about the factors driving regional integration in Europe that may account better for the cycles of stagnation and advance in European integration. In this other interpretation, the politics of national statesmen, politicians, and publics might be seen to play a larger role than they do in Wallace's account. This view would also bring into sharper focus the relevance of the European case to negotiations over political and economic convergence taking place elsewhere in the world.

From this alternative perspective the processes at work in the EC today may be seen to have much in common with those at work over years of negotiations between the United States and Japan (particularly as manifested in the Structural Impediment Initiative discussions); among the United States, Canada, and Mexico in the North

American Free Trade talks; and with many aspects of the debates over the Organization for Economic Cooperation and Development and the General Agreement on Tariffs and Trade. In all these cases we see recurrent negotiations among heavily interdependent societies over harmonization, convergence, and institution-building. Advances on these fronts are mainly driven by political demands for altering the regulation of economic interactions among nations. In *cool phases* it is the politics of the bureaucratic elites that prevail. As Wallace describes in the case of Europe, the principal actors are policy makers and trade negotiators socialized by long and intense participation in common problem-solving and joint management of zones of interaction and friction. In *hot phases* the national politicians predominate, and it is they who perceive and seize the opportunities that lead to big leaps forward in institution-building. Economic shifts—for example, the incentives provided to decisionmakers by larger markets; the new technologies of communication, transportation, and production—all do play roles. They create new stakes, new platforms for alliance and dissension. But they are neither imperatives nor drivers.

In pursuing this line of reasoning, one may agree with Wallace's insistence on how large the institutional-constitutional *acquis* is in Western Europe, after four decades of experience within this frame-work, in contrast to minimal "formal integration" in the North American or Asian regional cases. But one may wonder whether the processes of integration and convergence at work within Europe are radically different from those at work elsewhere in the world. Is the EU really a "proto-government" to be compared with the federal states of Canada and the United States? Are the days of independent European nation-states really over? Have they become, as Wallace claims, "post-modern states, which have moved on from traditional state functions of defense and territorial protection to more limited preoccupations with the partly collaborative, partly competitive pursuit of prosperity and welfare"? If one remembers the difficulties in reaching even minimal agreements on Yugoslavia—a conflict on the near-periphery of the Community, with many dangerous possibilities of spillover into Community territory—and the reversion to largely national decision-making, traditional state concerns hardly seem dead.[1]

---

1. Note Wallace's remarkably positive view of the European Community's record on Yugoslavia.

Consider the EC instead as a set of regional arrangements in which national governments retain many of their traditional prerogatives and in which deep public convictions about democratic legitimacy attach only to nation-states. From this perspective, interesting similarities appear between the political conflicts we see in Europe over changing domestic national practices and institutions in response to external norms and demands and conflicts over such issues among the United States, Japan, Mexico, Canada, and, increasingly, Korea, China, and others. The universe here might be defined as all those cases in which certain kinds of international economic exchange are made contingent on changes in national practices. Imagine European states, then, engaged in a long series of negotiations, in which the push and pull of anticipated economic and political gains produce a set of rules about how to regulate societal interdependence. Neither technological linkages nor economic logic dictates a single list of common activities that need to be harmonized. Rather, public perceptions of what constitutes fairness in economic exchange, elite understandings of how economies operate and gain competitive advantage, and much else come to make up the agenda of harmonization and integration. From such a perspective, the situation in Europe has much in common with that of countries seeking to regulate economic exchanges by creating new institutions and by reshaping domestic practices in other countries.

In Wallace's review of the history of European integration the starting point in the 1950s is political, a consensus among national statesmen, which is subsequently consolidated and stabilized by elite socialization and accelerated by a kind of economic spillover. The permissive condition is geographic propinquity. The process of integration Wallace then describes is a progressive, unidirectional, and cumulative one, a "learning process." Two mechanisms accelerate the process and keep it moving in the same direction. The first is a gradual socialization of bureaucratic elites through working together within European institutions and through an intensity of personal interaction with other bureaucrats that is facilitated by geography and improved transportation. Wallace attaches great importance to this process of elite acceptance of EC norms and procedures. From it is derived the elites' ability and willingness to implement EC decisions at the national level. Through elite socialization and the institutionalization of Community norms and implementation, the Community is gradually coming to supplant national governments. "Such a high degree of interpenetration of national governments carried with it a substantial disaggregation of the nation-state," he writes. "West European states cannot be seen in their relations with each other as coherent and coordinated entities negotiating over well-defined *national* interests."

The second mechanism at work in the process of integration is economic. Once transportation and communication links improved, "it made more sense for major manufacturers to produce and market on a European rather than a nation-by-nation basis. As they attempted to do so, the obstacles presented by separate national regulations became more and more burdensome." It seemed only reasonable to coordinate police and intelligence activities across borders. Once Europeans started operating more frequently outside their own countries, confronting border controls at each little country's frontiers seemed an "absurdity." "Affluent West Europeans had thus come by the 1980s to regard the western half of the continent, rather than their own national boundaries, as their relevant social space."

The high costs of subsidizing civil and military technology push states into collaborative research programs. The "electronic revolution . . . forced national governments into continuous consultations in new fields, fields that had previously been considered to fall within the realm of domestic policy." In sum, both economic incentives and a kind of inability of states to deal on a national basis with new aspects of the economy and new technologies led to the progressive hollowing out of the reality of national autonomy. Wallace concludes: "Economic and technological logic has swept away much of the traditional rationale for state autonomy within this densely packed international region."

But although the elites recognized these changes and accepted their implications, publics did not understand. The dilemma is not so much that the publics love their nation-states. On the contrary, in Wallace's view: people are quite disillusioned about the state's capacity to deal with even the ordinary problems of life. The dilemma is the absence of any popular political consensus on Europe as an alternative to the nation-state, hence a fragility of support, which was revealed in the Maastricht referenda votes and in a growing interest in separatist and regionalism movements. Therefore, in this view, the rock on which the European ship of state has crashed is political traditionalism: the public clinging out of habit rather than enthusiasm to a nineteenth-century concept of the nation, while economic logic commands new political structures.

There is much to think about in this account of the origins of European integration, which comes, indeed, at a time when a next generation of scholarship is reopening many of our conventional understandings of European construction.[2] Here I wish only to focus on the issue of how much weight in the explanation of the expansion of the Community can be borne by economic interests and economic interest groups. No one would deny that there were economic gains to be made—at least by some—in leveling national barriers to market access. Nor would any full account neglect the campaign for the single market mounted by heads of big European corporations; the role of arguments about the need for technological cooperation in the face of Japanese and American efforts; the influence of calculations like those presented in the Cecchini Report about the costs of non-Europe; and the many other ways in which economic interests and the perception of economic advantage mattered.

The question, though, is whether the integration process once engaged, for whatever reasons was essentially one driven by the spontaneous response of economic actors to perceived advantages in larger markets, these actors then dragging politicians along with them, or rather whether the process is best understood as one in which the main movers were political entrepreneurs. In the former interpretation, the process has a kind of natural momentum and unidirectionality from economic thrust, given shape and organizational coherence by enlightened, even if rather overburdened, technocrats. Wallace emphasizes more the bureaucratic shaping and the elements of continuity provided by the dense networks of elite interaction than the role of interest groups, but his account also finds the underlying motors accelerating integration to be economic and technological changes. In Wallace's interpretation, as in more narrowly economic accounts, politics is largely a drag factor, and at worst—as from 1992 onward—an irrational and retrograde phenomenon.

2. For examples of this new work, see Milward (1992) for a reinterpretation of the origins of the Community; on the European Court of Justice, recent work suggesting how different the Court's role has been from that of the Supreme Court in the U.S. federal system is presented in Alter and Meunier-Aitsahalia (1994).

From an alternative perspective, one might argue that the big push for European integration has always come from politics. The leaps forward in European integration and institution-building all followed from statesmen's changing perceptions of the opportunities for using EC expansion to resolve domestic political dilemmas. When François Mitterrand after 1983 had to jettison the programs associated with a socialist vision of the economy and decided on a major recommitment to Europe and to expansion of the European Community, he was responding not to economic opportunities or pressures, but to the political challenge of carving out a new program for the socialist party that could revive its sense of historic mission. After 1989, the German proposals for deepening the Community seem best understood as motivated by a need to reduce the European shock waves set off by reunification by pressing simultaneously for enlargement of the political responsibilities of European institutions. Even the Single Market Initiative of 1985 can be understood as a political response to a mounting sense of marginalization in face of American and Japanese power.[3]

From the perspective of these political interpretations, the advantages of economic scope and efficiency that might result from integration, the new electronic technologies, and new technologies of communication are facilitating factors, but hardly revolutionary in impact. Indeed, one might question just how much harmonization and integration *are* needed in economies in which leading-edge firms may no longer be those geared to mass production of standard commodities. Economies of scale are not the main issue for "multidomestic" firms like ABB, which focus on particular market segments and specialized customer demand, or for companies like Motorola, Toshiba, or Daimler-Benz, which are capable of making transnational alliances and which need to build a strong presence in all parts of the advanced industrial world.

The main strength of an interpretation of European integration in which politics plays a larger role would be to provide a consistent account of the fits and starts, the advances and reverses, of the integration process. The dynamic would not then pit economic logic against political irrationality. Rather, real changes in the domestic politics of European countries could be shown to produce changing

3. See Sandholtz and Zysman (1989).

assessments on the part of the elites of the domestic political advantages and disadvantages of various European strategies. Thus, for
example, whatever might be the objective "absurdities" of border
controls between neighboring small countries, the long-negotiated
Schengen Accord would be postponed sine die when intense public
concern over immigrant flows transformed public perceptions of this
agreement from a rationalizing technocratic measure into yet more
evidence of the state's letting down its guard on the frontiers of the
nation against dangerous intruders. The Schengen Accord was possible,
not because the public, in its new leisure travel across Europe, came to
chafe at the irrationality of border controls and to demand easier movement as a kind of consumer good. Rather, the accord was possible only
as long as the public was indifferent. Once the public focused on this
issue as yet another instance of European interference with the defense
of national prerogatives (i.e., limiting entry to national territory), politicians shelved it, although it had already been scheduled to go into effect.

From this perspective, 1992 does represent a sharp break. In the
past, the politics that had driven integration had been largely an affair
of elites, with the public apparently in favor of Europe, but in fact
mainly uninformed about its significance and uninterested.[4] The
Maastricht referenda campaigns for the first time catalyzed an enormous public debate over Europe and linked the extension of the EC's
authority to issues with real salience in everyday life. The result was
polarization, and even in France and Germany (countries in which
the public was believed to be strongly attached to Europe) only the
barest of majorities (as registered by votes in France and by survey-
takers in Germany) for the Maastricht Treaty.

Finally, to return to Wallace's interpretation of the European Community by the end of the 1980s and the early 1990s as a "proto-government": Is the United States really an appropriate point of comparison?
Even if we take with a grain of salt Wallace's affirmation that the
degree of implementation of EC directives and laws compares favor-
ably to that of U.S. federal law in southern United States fifty years
ago, are the mechanisms through which Community institutions
extend their authority in fact those on which the U.S. federal system
is based?[5] The basic difference lies in the stock of loyalties, commit-

---

4. For a prescient interpretation in this sense, see Percheron (1991).
5. See Alter and Meunier-Aitsahalia (1994).

ments and political identifications underpinning these political structures. American southerners of the 1940s did not contest the federal government's right to tax or to conscript them for a foreign war; in contrast, the European Community's legitimacy in regulating raw-milk cheese sales or bird hunting—let alone sending anyone into battle in Bosnia—is weak and contested. As Miles Kahler observed during discussion of this volume, in federal systems of government like those of the United States and Canada, the security and foreign policy domains were the first to be transferred to the federal government. Even under the weakest of federal systems, there is, he argued, nothing comparable to the "democratic deficit" of the European Community. The source of the weakness lies not so much in uneven implementation but in shaky foundations.

For these reasons it is difficult to agree with Wallace's assessment that European integration has disintegrated the nation-state. The legitimacy of the nation-states persists, despite rising levels of public distrust of officials and politicians and widespread disillusionment with the efficacy of public intervention in the economy. Anger against the politics of the national central governments in some places takes the form of support for regionalism and separatist movements, as Wallace points out. It also increasingly takes the form of an exacerbated nationalism as demonstrated by the phenomenal success of the anti-Maastricht coalition in France and the rise in that country of such politicians as Philippe Séguin, who proudly describes himself as a Jacobin. "The idea of frontiers is outdated! There's a dogma to attack! For bringing back the frontiers today is the condition of any policy."[6] "1992 is literally the anti-1789."[7] What we do not see is anger at the nation-state turning into greater public support and identification with Europe.

To put it another way, in Western Europe, as elsewhere in the world, the political meaning and the political fallout of economic interdependence are indeterminate. However challenged by the globalization of economic ROWS, the nation-state retains an undiminished legitimacy in the eyes of mass publics. Indeed the conjunction of rising global flows of capital with new immigrant flows across borders once politically closed has heightened sensitivities

6. Séguin (1993, pp. 47–48).
7. Séguin (1992, p. 17). On nationalist reactions against integration, see also Berger (1993).

everywhere to territorial facts, the control of frontiers, and national sovereignty. The lessons of the European experience are telling, precisely because, after almost forty years of community-building, the advances and retreats of deep integration continue to be regulated by nation-states.

Appendix: Institutions and Their Membership

European Economic Community, European Community, European Union

The European Community (EC) has evolved from the European Coal and Steel Community (ECSC) (Treaty of Paris, 1951), the European Economic Community (EEC), and the European Atomic Energy Community (Euratom) (Treaties of Rome, 1957). The Merger Treaty of 1965 integrated the High Authority of the ECSC and the two Commissions of EEC and Euratom; the three Communities continued to exist as separate legal entities, but in practice institutional structure and policymaking now operated within the framework of what was first known as "the European Communities," and gradually became "the European Community." Ratification of the Maastricht Treaty on European Union in 1993 brought the *European Community* within the broader framework of the *European Union,* which also included intergovernmental structures (the second and third "pillars") for cooperation in foreign and security policy and in justice and home affairs.

The six member states of the original three Communities were France, Federal Germany, Italy, Belgium, Luxembourg, and the Netherlands. The addition of Britain, Ireland, and Denmark raised membership to nine in 1973. (Norway also negotiated entry, but ratification of the treaty was rejected in a national referendum). Greece joined in 1981, and Portugal and Spain in 1986, to create an EC Twelve. Austria, Finland, Sweden, and Norway (again) completed negotiations for entry in early 1994, with the intention of completing ratification procedures for entry in 1995.

119

European Free Trade Association

The original seven member states that signed the Stockholm Convention of 1960 were Britain (its initiator), Denmark, Norway, Sweden, Austria, Switzerland, and Portugal. The Association (EFTA) was an explicitly intergovernmental organization, committed only to removal of barriers to industrial trade. Britain and Denmark defected to the EC in 1973; Finland and Iceland moved from association to full membership in the same year. Portugal moved to the EC in 1986, leaving an EFTA Six in the late 1980s to move toward a more active and group-to-group relationship with the EC, culminating in negotiations to establish a European Economic Area. A further complication is that tiny Lichtenstein, between Switzerland and Austria, declared its intentions to become a formal member of EFTA (and thus of the EEA also) in 1992. Therefore, for some purposes this principality of 35,000 people now acts as an additional EFTA member.

Western European Union

The Brussels Treaty was signed among Britain, France, Belgium, the Netherlands, and Luxembourg in 1948; its signatories brought their security ties within the wider Atlantic Alliance the following year. In 1954 the treaty was revised to bring in Federal Germany and Italy and extended to include British commitments on stationing troops in Germany and controls on German arms procurement. The Western European Union (WEU) entered into force in 1955. This seven-member WEU was enlarged to nine by Spanish and Portuguese accession in 1987. A protocol to the Maastricht Treaty brought the WEU within the framework of the European Union, offered membership to Greece, and created categories of observer status for the two other EU members (Denmark and Ireland) and association for other European members of the North Atlantic Treaty Organization (NATO) (Norway, Turkey, and Iceland). In 1992 the WEU followed NATO's initiative in establishing the NATO Consultative Committee (NACC) with the former Warsaw Pact countries by creating a parallel WEU Forum for Peace, with the crucial difference that NACC included Russia and the former Soviet republics (as well as the United States) whereas the WEU Forum brought the smaller states between

Germany and Russia into a security relationship with the members of the EU.

The original treaty contains a fifty-year review clause, which falls due in 1998. The future of the WEU and its potential integration with the EU will thus be on the agenda for the planned 1996 EU intergovernmental conference.

Council of Europe

Ten West European states (Britain, France, the Benelux countries, Italy, Norway, Sweden, Denmark, and Ireland) signed the Treaty of Westminster in 1949. Greece joined later that same year. The Council of Europe's structure was primarily intergovernmental, although it also included a consultative parliamentary assembly drawn from national parliaments. It was intended (by the Americans and by the more "committed" Europeans) to provide the political institutional structure for West European integration, complementing the economic structure provided by the Organization for European Economic Cooperation. Resistance from the British and Scandinavian governments to any suggestions of supranational authority or federalism in the development of the Council of Europe led the French, with active American support, to shift their attention the following year to the creation of a smaller and more integrated group, which became the European Coal and Steel Community.

By 1989 membership had grown to twenty-three, representing all European democratic states. Transition to democracy within the former Eastern Europe had enabled a further nine states to satisfy the criteria for membership by the beginning of 1994. Other states pressing to join had been granted "special guest" status; these included Russia and the Ukraine. In effect Council of Europe membership provides the certificate of democratic acceptability that qualifies European states to apply for membership in the European Community.

The Council of Europe's most visible activities are in the field of civil liberties; the European Commission for Human Rights and its associated court are part of this institutional structure. It has also drawn up European conventions on a range of functional issues, from standardization of road signs to educational exchange, and provides a framework for intergovernmental consultation on action against drugs, control of migration, and a range of other issues.

Conference on Security and Cooperation in Europe

The Conference (CSCE) began as the Helsinki conference of 1972–74, bringing together some thirty-one states from Western and Eastern Europe, together with the Soviet Union, the United States, and Canada, to negotiate a carefully linked series of bargains on military confidence-building, relaxation of restrictions on East-West trade and technology transfer, and standards of behavior for civil and human rights. The Final Act of that conference committed the signatories to keep under review the implementation of the obligations undertaken. A series of review conferences during the late 1970s and the 1980s provided for confrontations with East European states over backsliding on human rights and for more limited negotiations on other issues.

After 1989 there were hopes in Eastern and in Western Europe that the CSCE would develop into an all-European security organization. A small secretariat was established in Prague, and a European Ombudsman for Human Rights appointed. The outbreak of the Yugoslav conflict in 1991, however, demonstrated the fragility of the CSCE's institutional structure and influence and led to the diversion of the security dialogue between West and East European countries into the NACC and the WEU Forum.

Upon the breakup of the Soviet Union all of its successor states applied to join the CSCE. This influx has raised its membership above fifty—a number that is still rising as new states emerging from the breakup of Yugoslavia and the Soviet Union are admitted. Little attention has been paid to ethnic and military conflicts in the Caucasus and central Asia, although the Ombudsman for Human Rights has played a conciliatory role in relation to Russian minorities within the Baltic states.

Europe Agreements

Europe Agreements have been negotiated by the European Community with a number of former socialist states, as the latter press toward EC membership. The EC initially resisted an explicit acknowledgment that ratification of such agreements represented the first step toward full membership; however, after intense lobbying from these states and pressure within the EC from the German government, the Copenhagen European Council of June 1993 accepted this interpretation. The Agreements allow for gradual moves toward free trade, subject to extensive safeguards (most particularly in agriculture, textiles, and steel), and for financial transfers to the associated states.

Poland, Hungary, and Czechoslovakia (thereafter labeled the "Visegrad" countries, after the site of a joint declaration by the three governments on relations with the EC) signed the first Europe Agreements in December 1991. Those with Poland and Hungary came into force on February 1, 1994; the Czech Republic and Slovakia had meanwhile signed again as separate states in October 1993. Romania signed in February 1993, Bulgaria in October. EC governments were preparing a negotiating mandate for talks with Slovenia in the summer of 1994. The three Baltic states (Estonia, Latvia, and Lithuania) had implicitly been accepted as candidates for future Europe Agreements—and thus for eventual EC membership. Their free trade agreements with the Nordic countries, however, enabled the EC to deal with them for the time being as a subset of the EFTA enlargement negotiations.

References

Aaron, Henry, and others. 1992. "Integrating the World Economy." Memo. Brookings.

Albert, Michel. 1993. *Capitalism against Capitalism.* London: Whurr.

Aldrich, Richard. 1994. "European Integration, Political Elites and the American Intelligence Connection." In *European Construction: National Decision-makers and Post-war European Institution-building,* edited by Anne Deighton. London: Macmillan.

Alter, Karen J., and Sophie Meunier-Aitsahalia. 1994. "Judicial Politics in the European Community: European Integration and the Pathbreaking Cassis de Dijon Decision." *Comparative Political Studies* 26(4): 535–61.

Anderson, Malcolm, and den Boer, Monica, eds. 1994. *Policing across National Boundaries.* London: Pinter.

Asia-Pacific Economic Cooperation. 1993. *A Vision for APEC: Towards an Asia-Pacific Economic Community.* Report of the Eminent Persons Group to APEC ministers (October).

Berger, Suzanne. 1993. "The Coming Protectionism: Or Why France, a Country with a Trade Surplus, Sees Foreign Trade as a Source of Rising Unemployment." Paper presented at the conference "The New France in a New Europe," Center for German and European Studies, Georgetown University, Washington, D.C., October 22–24.

Bull, Hedley. 1982. "Civilian Power Europe: A Contradiction in Terms?" *Journal of Common Market Studies* 21(1–2): 149–64.

Burley, Anne-Marie, and Walter Mattli. 1993. "Europe before the Court: A Political Theory of Legal Integration." *International Organization* 47(Winter): 41–76.

Cleveland, Harold B. van. 1966. *The Atlantic Idea and Its European Rivals.* McGraw-Hill.

Commission of the European Communities. 1994. *Eleventh Annual Report on Monitoring the Application of Community Law.* Brussels: COM(94) 500, 29.03.1994.

Den Boer, Monica, and Neil Walker. 1993. "European Policing after 1992." *Journal of Common Market Studies* 31(1): 3–28.

125

De Schoutheete, Philippe. 1986. *La Coopération Politique Européene.* 2d ed. Brussels: Labor.

———. 1991. "The European Community and Its Sub-Systems" in *The Dynamics of European Integration,* edited by William Wallace, 106–124. London: Pinter.

Deutsch, Karl W., and others. 1957. *Political Community and the North Atlantic Area: International Organization in the Light of Historical Experience.* Princeton University Press.

Duroselle, Jean-Baptiste. 1990. *Europe: A History of Its Peoples.* London: Viking.

EFTA Secretariat, Press and Information Service. 1993. *The EEA Agreement.* Geneva.

Ellwood, David W. 1992. *Rebuilding Europe: Western Europe, America, and Postwar Reconstruction.* London: Longman.

European Institute of Public Administration. 1991. *Subsidiarity: The Challenge of Change: Proceeding of the Jacques Delors Colloquim.* Maastricht: EIPA.

Evans, Peter B., Harold K. Jacobson, and Robert D. Putnam, eds. 1993. *Double-edged Diplomacy: International Bargaining and Domestic Politics.* University of California at Berkeley Press.

Forster, Anthony, Anand Menon, and William Wallace. 1992. "A Common European Defence?' *Survival* (September–October): 98–118.

Garcia, Soledad, ed. 1993. *European Identity and the Search for Legitimacy.* London: Pinter.

Gladwyn, Lord. 1966. *The European Idea.* London: Weidenfeld and Nicolson.

Green, Maria. 1993. "The Politics of Big Business in the Single Market Program." Paper presented at European Community Studies Association Conference, Washington, D.C., May 27, 1993.

Grosser, Alfred. 1980. *The Western Alliance: European-American Relations since 1945.* London: Macmillan.

Haas, Ernst B. 1958. *The Uniting of Europe: Political, Social, and Economic Forces, 1950–57.* Stanford University Press.

———. 1961. "International Integration: The European and the Universal Process." *International Organization* 15(Summer): 366–92.

Hallstein, Walter. 1973. *Europe in the Making.* New York: Norton.

Hogan, Michael J. 1987. *The Marshall Plan: America, Britain and the Reconstruction of Western Europe, 1947–1952.* Cambridge University Press.

Judt, Tony. 1992. "The Past Is Another Country: Myth and Memory in Postwar Europe." *Daedalus* 121(Fall): 83–118.

Kelstrup, Morten, ed. 1992. *European Integration and Denmark's Participation.* Copenhagen Political Studies Press.

Keohane, Robert O. 1984. *After Hegemony: Cooperation and Discord in the World Political Economy.* Princeton University Press.

Keynes, John Maynard. 1919. *The Economic Consequences of the Peace.* London: Macmillan.

Kissinger, Henry. 1982. *Years of Upheaval.* London: Weidenfeld and Nicolson.

Koh, Harold Hongju. 1991. "Transnational Public Law Litigation." *Yale Law Journal* 100(June): 2347–401.

Liebfried, Stefan. 1992. "Europe's Would-Be Social State: Social Policy in Europe after 1992." In *Singular Europe: Economy and Polity of the European Community after 1992*, edited by William James Adams. University of Michigan Press.

Mearsheimer, John J. 1990. "Back to the Future: Instability in Europe after the Cold War." *International Security* 15(Summer): 5–56.

Michalski, Anna, and Helen Wallace. 1992. *The European Community: The Challenge of Enlargement*. London: Royal Institute of International Affairs.

Milward, Alan. 1992. *The European Rescue of the Nation-State*. London: Routledge.

Milward, Alan S., and others. 1993. *The Frontier of National Sovereignty: History and Theory 1945–1992*. London: Routledge.

Mitrany, David. 1943. *A Working Peace System: An Argument for the Functional Development of International Organization*. New York: Oxford University Press.

Nye, Joseph S., Jr. 1990. *Bound to Lead: The Changing Nature of American Power*. Basic Books.

O'Keeffe, David. 1993. "The Agreement on the European Economic Area." In *Yearbook of European Law, 1992*, edited by F. G. Jacobs, 1–27. New York: Oxford University Press.

Paarlberg, Robert. 1994. *Leadership Abroad Begins at Home: U.S. Foreign Economic Policy after the Cold War*. Brookings.

Palmer, Michael, and others. 1968. *European Unity: A Survey of European Organizations*. London: Allen and Unwin.

Pelkmans, Jacques, L. Alan Winters, and Helen Wallace. 1988. *Europe's Domestic Market*. London: Routledge.

Percheron, Annick. 1991. "Les Français et l'Europe. Acquiescement de Façade ou Adhésion Véritable." *Revue Française de Science Politique* 41(3): 382–406.

Pinder, John. 1968. "Positive Integration and Negative Integration: Some Problems of Economic Union in the EC." *The World Today* 24(March): 88–110.

Press and Information Service, Efta Secretariat, Geneva, 1993. *The EEA Agreement*.

Putnam, Robert D., and Nicholas Bayne. 1987. *Hanging Together: Cooperation and Conflict in the Seven-Power Summits*, revised ed. London: Sage.

Rijksbaron, Albert, and others. 1987. *Europe from a Cultural Perspective: Historiography and Perceptions*. The Hague: Nijgh & Van Ditmar Universitair.

Romero, Federico. 1991. "Cross-Border Population Movements." In *The Dynamics of European Integration*, edited by William Wallace, 171–91. London: Pinter.

———. 1993. "Italy and the Politics of Migration." In *The Frontier of National Sovereignty: History and Theory 1945–1992*, edited by Alan S. Milward. London: Routledge.

Rosenthal, Douglas E., and William M. Knighton. 1982. *National Laws and International Commerce: The Problem of Extra-Territoriality*. London: Routledge.

Sandholtz, Wayne. 1992. *High-Tech Europe: The Politics of International Cooperation*. University of California at Berkeley Press.

Sandholtz, Wayne, and John Zysman. 1989. "1992: Recasting the European Bargain." *World Politics* 42 (October): 95–128.

Scharpf, Fritz W. 1988. "The Joint-Decision Trap: Lessons from German Federalism and European Integration." *Public Administration* 66(Autumn): 239–78.

Schlesinger, Philip. 1991. "Media, the Political Order and National Identity." *Media, Culture and Society* 13(July): 297–308.

Séguin, Philippe. 1992. *Discours pour la France.* Paris: Grasset.

———. 1993. *Ce que J'ai Dit.* Paris: Grasset.

Sharp, Margaret, and Claire Shearman. 1987. *European Technological Collaboration.* London: Routledge.

Shonfield, Andrew. 1965. *Modern Capitalism: The Changing Balance of Public and Private Power.* New York: Oxford University Press.

Smith, Alasdair, and Helen Wallace. 1994. "The European Union: Towards a Policy for Europe." *International Affairs* 70(3): 1–16.

Smith, Anthony D. 1991. *National Identity.* London: Penguin.

———. 1992. "National Identity and the Idea of European Unity." *International Affairs* 68(January): 55–76.

Thurow, Lester. 1992. *Head to Head: The Coming Economic Battle among Japan, Europe, and America.* Morrow.

Tuchman, Barbara W. 1966. *The Proud Tower: A Portrait of the World before the War, 1890–1914.* Macmillan.

Urwin, Derek W. 1991. *The Community of Europe: A History of European Integration since 1945.* New York: Longman.

Wallace, Helen. 1989. "The Best Is the Enemy of the Could: Bargaining in the European Community." In *Agricultural Trade Liberalization and the European Community,* edited by Secondo Tarditi and others, 193–206. Oxford: Clarendon Press.

———. 1991a. "Making Multilateral Negotiations Work." In *The Dynamics of European Integration,* edited by William Wallace, 213–28. London: Pinter.

———, ed. 1991b. *The Wider Western Europe: Reshaping the EC/EFTA Relationship.* London: Pinter.

Wallace, Helen, and Adam Ridley. 1985. *Europe, the Challenge of Diversity.* London: Royal Institute of International Affairs.

Wallace, William. 1976. "Issue Linkage among Atlantic Governments." *International Affairs* 52(April): 163–79.

———1984. *Britain's Bilateral Links within Western Europe.* London: Routledge.

———. 1986. "What Price Independence? Sovereignty and Interdependence in British Politics." *International Affairs* 62(Summer): 367–89.

———. 1990. *The Transformation of Western Europe.* New York: Council on Foreign Relations Press.

———, ed. 1991a. *The Dynamics of European Integration.* London: Pinter.

———. 1991b. "Foreign Policy and National Identity in the United Kingdom." *International Affairs.* 67(January): 65–80.

———. 1992. "British Foreign Policy after the Cold War." *International Affairs.* 68(July): 423–42.

———. 1994. "Rescue or Retreat? The Nation State in Western Europe, 1945–93." *Political Studies* 42 (special issue, "The Crisis of the Nation State").

Wallace, William, and David Allen. 1977. "Political Cooperation: Procedure as Substitute for Policy." in *Policy-making in the European Communities,* edited by Helen Wallace, William Wallace, and Carole Webb, 227–48. Wiley.

Webb, Carole. 1983. "Theoretical Perspectives and Problems." In *Policy-making in the European Community,* 2d ed., edited by Helen Wallace, William Wallace, and Carole Webb, 1–42. Wiley.

Weidenfeld, Werner. 1984. "Was ist die Idee Europas?" *Aus Politik- und Zeitgeschichte* (June): 5–12.

Weiler, Joseph. 1982. "Community Member States and European Integration: Is the Law Relevant?" *Journal of Common Market Studies* 21(1–2): 39–56.

———. 1991. "The transformation of Europe." *Yale Law Journal* 100(June): 2403–84.

Weiss, Friedl. 1991. "The Legal Issues." In *The Wider Western Europe: Reshaping the EC/EFTA Relationship,* edited by Helen Wallace, 246–67. London: Pinter.

Wessels, Wolfgang. 1991a. "Administrative Interaction." In *The Dynamics of European Integration,* edited by William Wallace, 229–41. London: Pinter.

———. 1991b. "The EC Council: The Community's Decisionmaking Center." In *The New European Community: Decisionmaking and Institutional Change,* edited by Robert O. Keohane and Stanley Hoffmann, 133–54. Boulder, Colorado: Westview Press.

Wijkman, Per Magnus. 1991. "Patterns of Production and Trade." In *The Dynamics of European Integration,* edited by William Wallace, 89–105. London: Pinter.

Wilke, Marc, and Helen Wallace. 1990. Subsidiarity: Approaches to Power-sharing in the European Community. Discussion Paper 27. London: Royal Institute of International Affairs.

Woolcock, Stephen. 1992. *Trading Partners or Trading Blows: Market Access in EC-US Relations.* New York: Council on Foreign Relations.

Index